The Good Humor Book

The Good Humor Book

COMPILED BY
ROLAND PETERSON

VISION HOUSE PUBLISHERS
Santa Ana, California 92705

The Good Humor Book

Santa Ana, California 92705

Library of Congress Catalog Card No. 76-52546
ISBN 0-88449-060-2

Printed in the United States of America.

CONTENTS

This book is dedicated to my wife, Kiva, and my three children, Linda, Louanne, and Danny, who have made my life worthwhile. Happiness and a sense of humor go hand-in-hand. I've made a good living, but they've made my living good!

INTRODUCTION

If you're looking for a book of sexy jokes or off-color stories, you might as well save your money. This book contains only material that would not offend the dearest of saints. My contention is that humor can be clean and that Satan doesn't have a corner on laughter or fun. Living in a wonderful country and enjoying a wholesome, good life has given me many reasons to be grateful. I have every reason to be happy, and I believe a sense of humor is a great asset that we need to have and can have.

As we journey through life we are beset by trials, troubles, and tribulations. God has given us many senses, one of which is a sense of humor. It is my desire as you read this book that you will be able to crowd out of your minds the problems and troubles which so easily beset us, and that you will be able to enjoy some heartfelt laughs and some challenging bits of wisdom. Life is too short not to enjoy it to the fullest. Smile often—it raises your face value. Remember, we don't stop laughing when we grow old—we grow old when we stop laughing.

HUMOR INDEX

Chapter I

QUICKIES

DID YOU HEAR ABOUT ...

... the clever cat who ate some cheese and breathed down the rat hole with baited breath?

★ ★ ★

... the traveling salesman by the name of Tony whose wife made him quit his job? it seems she wanted her Tony home permanent.

★ ★ ★

... the naughty little kangaroo who ran away from home and left his mother holding the bag?

★ ★ ★

... the bee that got mad because somebody took his honey and nectar?

★ ★ ★

... Mickey Mouse? He ran away from home because he found out his father was a rat.

★ ★ ★

... the snake who gave birth to a bouncing baby boa?

. . . the despondent cockroach who committed insecticide?

★ ★ ★

. . . the Chinese cook who died after eating some of his own cooking? The papers listed it as chop sueycide.

★ ★ ★

. . . the fellow who cast his bread upon the waters? He was arrested for polluting.

★ ★ ★

. . . the religious moth who gave up woolens for lint?

GOOD NEWS, BAD NEWS

"I have some good news and some bad news for you"—

★ ★ ★

The good news—Your son just broke the Olympic diving record for the triple somersault from the high board.
The bad news—There was no water in the pool.

The good news—I spotted the first robin of Spring.
The bad news—He spotted me first.

The good news—You've made the Olympic javelin team.
The bad news—Your job is to catch the javelin.

★ ★ ★

The good news—We just sold your millionth record.
The bad news—We still can't get rid of the first 999,999.

★ ★ ★

The good news—I just got you a job with the circus. You'll have to be willing to travel but I think you're the man with the right caliber.
The bad news—You're going to be the new Human Cannonball.

★ ★ ★

The doctor said to his patient, "I've got some good news and some bad news for you. The bad news is that I amputated the wrong leg. The good news is that your bad leg is getting better."

DAFFYNITIONS

Pro wrestler—A struggling actor.

★ ★ ★

Gourmet—A glutton who owns a dress suit.

★ ★ ★

Oldtimer—A person who remembers when there was something behind the old red schoolhouse besides the PTA.

Family swimming pool—a small body of water surrounded by other people's kids.

Dandelion—Pretty good fibbing.

Rawhide—Something you have after a hard spanking.

Dad burnit—Dad's cooking.

Kibitzer—A person with an interferiority complex.

Masseur—A person who leaves no stern untoned.

Golddigger—A woman who runs her hands through a man's hair so she can later run them through his money.

Kleenex—Your daily nose-paper.

Press agent—One who has hitched his braggin' to a star.

Underrate—Seven.

★ ★ ★

Weasel—It blows at noon.

★ ★ ★

Gland—The only thing secretive about a woman.

★ ★ ★

Navel destroyer—A hula hoop with a nail in it.

SIGNS OF THE TIMES

AUTO REPAIR SHOP—"May We Have the Next Dents?"

★ ★ ★

DIVORCE LAWYER'S DOOR—"Satisfaction Guaranteed or Your Honey Back "

★ ★ ★

BLOOD BANK—"Let's Not Get Caught with Our Pints Down"

★ ★ ★

GATE OF A NUDIST COLONY—"Clothed for the Winter Months"

★ ★ ★

ZIPPER DISPLAY—"Grand Opening Sale"

FIREPLACE ACCESSORIES—"Anything Your Little Hearth Desires"

★ ★ ★

CANOE RENTAL SHOP—"No Tipping Allowed"

★ ★ ★

SCHOOL OFFICE—"Bored of Education"

★ ★ ★

AT BEACH—"A Coat of Tan is Yours for the Basking"

★ ★ ★

BATTERY SHOP—"The Only Place in Town Where Everybody Can Charge It"

SHOW ME...

. . . an arrogant insect, and I'll show you a cocky roach.

★ ★ ★

. . . a squirrel's home, and I'll show you a nutcracker's suite.

★ ★ ★

. . . a lazy butcher, and I'll show you a meat loafer.

★ ★ ★

. . . a broken record, and I'll show you a smash hit.

★ ★ ★

. . . a dead ringer, and I'll show you a deceased Avon lady.

★ ★ ★

. . . a dressmaker, and I'll show you a person who knows the seamy side of life.

★ ★ ★

. . . a man getting a smallpox injection from a cheerful nurse, and I'll show you a man taking a friendly needling.

★ ★ ★

. . . a guy who has given up drinking, and I'll show you a guy who did it for his wife and kidneys.

★ ★ ★

. . . a fellow who has kissed the blarney stone, and I'll show you a fellow with a sex problem.

TWOSOMES

Englishman: "King William struck my ancestor on the shoulder with his sword and made a knight out of him."

American: "That's nothing. Sitting Bull hit my grandfather on the head with a tomahawk and made an angel out of him."

Moe: "I hear the administration is trying to stop necking in the halls."
Joe: "Is that so?"
Moe: "Yeah! The first thing you know, they'll be trying to make the students stop, too."

Jack: "Suppose you were in a car all by yourself and a gang of hoodlums followed you at 75 miles per hour. What would you do?"
Pete: "At least 85."

Bill: "Did you hear about the fellow who almost went blind drinking a cup of coffee?"
Jake: "No, how come?"
Bill: "He left the spoon in the cup."

Lenny: "How did you hurt your arm?"
Benny: "See that big rock over there?"
Lenny: "Yes."
Benny: "Well, I didn't!"

Older brother: "Why are you wearing my new raincoat?"
Younger brother: "I didn't want to get your new sport coat wet."

Hostess: "Our dog is just like one of the family."
Guest: "Yes, I can see the resemblance."

MORE DAFFYNITIONS

Baby—Mama's little yelper.

★ ★ ★

Hula dancer—A shake in the grass.

★ ★ ★

Bigamist—Severe fog in Naples.

★ ★ ★

Abalone—An expression of disbelief.

★ ★ ★

Archeologist—A man whose career lies in ruins.

★ ★ ★

Castor Oil—Ugh nog.

★ ★ ★

Debate—What attracts de fish.

★ ★ ★

Flood—A stream too big for its bridges.

★ ★ ★

Panic—Kiss the Poise good-by.

★ ★ ★

Vice Versa—Poetry not fit for the kids to read.

★ ★ ★

Summer—When parents pack up their troubles and send them off to camp.

★ ★ ★

Seersucker—A gullible fortuneteller.

★ ★ ★

Gruesome—A little taller than last year.

I COULD HAVE BEEN . . .

. . . a parachutist, but nothing ever opened up.

★ ★ ★

. . . a truck driver, but I just couldn't go that route.

★ ★ ★

. . . a bank robber, but I got alarmed.

★ ★ ★

. . . an author, but it just wasn't write for me.

★ ★ ★

. . . a trapeze artist, but I couldn't get the hang of it.

★ ★ ★

. . . a violinist, but I was too high-strung.

★ ★ ★

. . . a professional bowler, but it wasn't up my alley.

★ ★ ★

. . . a magician, but the urge suddenly vanished.

★ ★ ★

. . . a librarian, but I shelved that idea.

★ ★ ★

. . . a plumber, but that was just a pipe dream.

★ ★ ★

. . . a window-washer, but I was all washed up.

★ ★ ★

. . . a policeman, but I suddenly copped out.

★ ★ ★

. . . an elevator operator, but I felt the job has too many ups and downs.

★ ★ ★

. . . a butcher, but I couldn't make ends meet.

★ ★ ★

SILLIES ...

A farmer increased egg production by putting up this sign in his hen house—"An egg a day keeps Colonel Sanders away."

The idea for daylight-saving time came from an old Indian chief who cut off one end of his blanket and had it sewed on the other end to make the blanket longer.

A chrysanthemum by any other name would be a lot easier to spell.

A hamburger by any other name costs twice as much.

I know one nightclub joint where the music is so bad that when a waiter dropped a tray full of dishes one night, everyone got up and started dancing.

She's still just as pretty, but it takes her half-an-hour longer now.

My son is at an awkward age—too young to leave home alone and too old to trust with a baby-sitter.

Bill: "How do you teach a lady to swim?"
Mark: "Put your arms around her gently, take her hand in yours, and put—"
Bill: "Wait a minute, this is my sister."
Mark: "Aw, throw her off the dock."

★ ★ ★

"Isn't it great to be speeding like this, mile after mile? Doesn't it make you glad to be alive?"
"Glad? I'm amazed."

★ ★ ★

Chemistry teacher: "This gas contains deadly poison. What steps would you take if it escaped?"
Student: "Long ones, sir!"

MORE SIGNS OF THE TIMES

TAILOR SHOP—As ye sew, so shall ye rip.

★ ★ ★

DOG KENNEL—Chock Full O Mutts.

★ ★ ★

LOCKSMITH—Let me help you out or in.

★ ★ ★

MUSIC STORE—Come in, pick out a drum, then beat it.

★ ★ ★

PUBLIC RELATIONS FIRM—We'll never give your feat a rest.

★ ★ ★

SEA FOOD CAFE—Our fish come from the best schools.

★ ★ ★

AGRICULTURAL SCHOOL—We till it like it is.

★ ★ ★

TRAVEL AGENCY—Let us show you our latest bag of treks.

★ ★ ★

GARDEN SHOP—There's a fungus among us—let us spray.

★ ★ ★

FINANCE COMPANY—In financial deep water? Loans made while you wade.

★ ★ ★

MOTEL—Inn mates wanted.

★ ★ ★

BAKERY—We discovered our roll in life.

★ ★ ★

CUSTOMS OFFICE—Customs inspectors know their duties.

DOWN ALONG THE HIGHWAY

Remember the Burma Shave Signs?

★ ★ ★

His face was smooth and cool as ice,
and oh, Louise, he smelled so nice.

★ ★ ★

At school crossings please go slow,
let our little shavers grow.

★ ★ ★

He had the ring, he had the flat,
but she felt his face, and that was that.

★ ★ ★

The whale put Jonah down the hatch,
but coughed him up because he scratched.

★ ★ ★

If at first you don't suceed
try a little ardor.

★ ★ ★

No lady likes to dance or dine,
accompanied by a porcupine.

★ ★ ★

The bearded lady tried a jar;
she's now a famous movie star.

If in heaven we don't meet,
remember Burma Shave beats the heat.

MORE DAFFYNITIONS

Credit cards—Due unto others what my wife gets a charge out of.

★ ★ ★

Sandwich spread—What you get from eating between meals.

★ ★ ★

Inflation—When you can't make one end meet.

★ ★ ★

Twins—Infant replay.

★ ★ ★

Career girl—One who'd rather bring home the bacon than fry it.

★ ★ ★

Gladiator—What the cannibal said after he ate the female explorer.

★ ★ ★

Inflation—Something that cost $10 to buy a few years ago and now costs $20 to repair.

★ ★ ★

Jaywalking—An exercise that brings on that run-down feeling.

★ ★ ★

Procrastinator—Man with a wait problem.

★ ★ ★

Small fry—A one-dollar steak.

★ ★ ★

Sneezing—Much achoo about nothing.

★ ★ ★

Taxidermist—A man who knows his stuff.

★ ★ ★

Violin—A bad hotel.

★ ★ ★

Credit card—The sweet buy-and-buy.

★ ★ ★

Husband—A fellow who believes that his wife's constant chattering is just one of life's little earitations.

★ ★ ★

Inflation—A drop in the buck.

★ ★ ★

BUSINESS REPORTS YOU'LL NEVER SEE ON WALL STREET

ASTRONOMER—My business is looking up.

★ ★ ★

GERMAN BUTCHER—Mine couldn't be wurst—and that's no baloney.

★ ★ ★

CIGAR MAKER—Mine is going up in smoke.

★ ★ ★

AUTHOR—Mine is all write.

★ ★ ★

TAILOR—Mine is just sew, sew.

★ ★ ★

FARMER—Mine is growing.

★ ★ ★

ELECTRIC COMPANY—Ours is pretty light.

★ ★ ★

TRASH COLLECTORS—Ours is picking up.

★ ★ ★

OPTICIAN—Mine is looking better.

DYNAMITE COMPANY—Ours is booming.

★ ★ ★

BANANA GROWERS—Ours is slipping.

★ ★ ★

RUBBER COMPANY—Ours is expanding.

★ ★ ★

ELEVATOR COMPANY—Ours is up and then it's down.

★ ★ ★

TRANSFER COMPANY—Our business is moving.

★ ★ ★

CLOCK COMPANY—Oh, we have our moments.

★ ★ ★

EGG PRODUCER—It's not all that it's cracked up to be.

★ ★ ★

SUGAR PRODUCER—Things are going real sweet.

★ ★ ★

BETTY CROCKER—Business is really stirring.

★ ★ ★

BEE KEEPER—It's a honey of a business.

Chapter 2

HERE AND THERE

A woman shopping for a present for her husband was determined to get him out of the stodgy, conservative clothing he had always bought for himself. So she said to the saleswoman in the menswear section of the store, "I'm looking for something wild and youthful in a pair of men's slacks."

The saleswoman sighed and replied, "Aren't we all, dearie, aren't we all?"

★ ★ ★

Once two hunters got lost in the forest. The first hunter said, "Now we must be calm." The second hunter agreed, "You're right. I once read that if you get lost you should shoot three times into the air and someone will come and rescue you."

So they did this, but nothing happened. They did it again, but still no help came. They repeated this several times without results. Finally the first hunter said, "What are we going to do now?" And the second hunter replied, "I don't know. We're almost out of arrows."

★ ★ ★

One day in ancient Roman times 50 slaves on a rowing boat were listening intently to the slavemaster as he was making an announcement. "O.K., men, today we've got some good news and some bad news. First the good news: each of you is getting a double ration of cold water. Now the bad news. After lunch you've really got to pull on those oars. The captain wants to go water skiing."

★ ★ ★

A student was explaining his poor grades to his irate father. "You just can't beat the system, Dad. Last semester I decided to take basket-weaving. It's a snap course and I figured I would sail through. Know what happened? Two Navajos enrolled, raised the class average, and I flunked."

★ ★ ★

A sergeant had a squad of recruits out for rifle practice, and he was disgusted with their poor shooting, especially that of one of the men.

"Say," he said to one of the sorriest specimens, "you're the bummest shot in the whole regiment. You're no good at long-range work, you're rotten at the short range, and you're even worse at medium. I don't believe you can hit anything. The best thing you can do is go behind those bushes and shoot yourself."

The recruit said nothing, and the sergeant turned his attention to the other men. In a few minutes he heard a shot from behind the bushes. He rushed over, with visions of the recruit lying dead from a suicide shot. But as he got there, the rookie stood up and greeted him with a sheepish grin: "It's all right, sergeant; I missed again."

★ ★ ★

Joe had a cat he loved very much. When he went west to California on a business trip he left the cat with his brother Al and his mother. When Joe arrived in Los Angeles he called his brother and asked him how the cat was doing. Al replied bluntly, "I'm real sorry, Joe, but your cat is dead."

Brokenhearted, Joe said, "How could you be so cruel? You know how I loved that cat. You could have said, 'Your cat is up on the roof and we can't get her down!' Then the next time I called you could have told me, 'Your cat is off the roof but it has broken a small bone in its leg and is in the hospital.' "

"Then a few days later, when I was better prepared, you could have called and said, 'Your cat has passed away in her sleep. She felt no pain.' "

"You're right," replied Al meekly. "I'm real sorry how about how it was handled. Please forgive me."

A couple of weeks later Joe once again called his brother from California. After chatting for awhile he asked, "Say, Al, how's Mother?"

"Oh, Mother?" responded Al, "O.K., I guess, but she's up on the roof and we can't get her down. . . ."

Two old retired buddies from Sun City went fishing together one day. For three hours neither moved a muscle. Then one got a bit restless. "Confound it, Joe," grumbled the other, "That's the second time you've shifted your feet in the past forty minutes. Did you come out here to fish or to dance?"

★ ★ ★

Informing the passengers on a jet that some turbulence was expected shortly, the stewardess ordered seatbelts to be buckled, then passed out sticks of chewing gum. A very proper dame announced. "I never touch chewing gum," but the stewardess told her, "We're going up to 30,000 feet, and the gum definitely will keep your ears from popping at such a high altitude."

Just before the plane landed in Los Angeles, the lady summoned the stewardess in some embarrassment. "My two grandchildren are waiting to meet me," she said. "How do I get this confounded gum out of my ears?"

★ ★ ★

Two goats found an old container of movie film. One of the goats nuzzled the can until the lid came off, and the other goat loosened the spool and ate a few frames.

The second goat ate some too, and soon they had eaten the whole film. When nothing was left but the can and the spool, the first goat said, "Wasn't that great?"

"Oh, I don't know," replied the second goat. "I thought the book was better!"

★ ★ ★

There's the story about the woman who divorced her husband and obtained custody of their 12-year-old son. When she remarried after a year or so, her ex-husband was somewhat concerned about the boy. On one of the visiting weekends the boy's father asked his son, "How do you get along with your stepfather?"

"Fine," said the youngster. "He takes me swimming every morning. We go to the lake, he rows me out to the middle, and then I swim back in."

"Isn't that a pretty long swim for a boy of your age?" asked the father.

"Not too bad. Really, the only tough part of it is getting out of the burlap bag."

★ ★ ★

Two men went after the same cab. After a short discussion one of them returned to his wife at the curb.

"Why did you let him have that cab?" she asked.

"He needed it more than I did," replied her husband. "Besides, he was late for his karate class."

The lady passenger became hysterical when she saw the flames licking engines one and two. "We're on fire!" she shouted up and down the aisles. "We're on fire! We're going to crash!" The entire planeload of passengers was in panic.

Suddenly the pilot appeared wearing a parachute. "Please be calm, everyone; don't worry about a thing," he assured them as he opened the door and stepped out with a parachute. "I'm going for help."

★ ★ ★

One of two women riding on a bus suddenly realized she had failed to pay her fare. "I'll go right up and pay it," she declared.

"Why bother?" her friend replied. "You got away with it—so what?"

"I've found honesty always pays," said the first woman virtuously, and went up to pay the driver. When she returned to her seat she exclaimed, "See, I told you honesty pays. I handed the driver a quarter and he gave me change for 50 cents."

★ ★ ★

On a city bus one evening, a woman was bothering the driver every few minutes to remind her when to get off.

"How will I know when we get to my street?" she asked for the umpteenth time.

The bus driver couldn't resist replying, "By the big smile on my face, lady!"

ANIMAL CRACKERS

Larry: "I went to the zoo yesterday and got in trouble."

Jack: "How did you get in trouble?"

Larry: "I fed a monkey."

Jack: "How did you get in trouble by feeding a monkey?"

Larry: "I fed a monkey to a lion."

★ ★ ★

Two kangaroos were talking to each other, and one said, "Gee, I hope it doesn't rain today. I just hate it when the kids play inside."

★ ★ ★

The hippopotamus was next to the giraffe in the zoo. The giraffe peered over the fence and said to the hippo, "Boy, I sure feel lousy. I have a sore throat. It's killing me!"

The hippo exclaimed, "You think you've got troubles! I have chapped lips."

★ ★ ★

One dragon said to another, "Why do you sleep in the daytime?"

"It's simple," replied his dragon friend; "I like to hunt knights."

Two elephants were cruising through the dense jungle when Jumbo stumbled over a hidden log and broke his big toe. His buddy came back to console him, but Jumbo blurted out, "Don't just stand there, stupid; go get a big toe truck!"

Ned: "I crossed an ant with a lion."
Zed: "What did you get?"
Ned: "I don't know, but it's going to be some picnic."

HERE AND THERE AGAIN

It happened on Highway 89. A man in a sports car was cruising along at about 90 MPH when a policeman stopped him and growled, "Say, Buddy, didn't you see the speed limit sign back there?"

"Why, yes, officer," replied the speeder, "I thought it said 89 miles an hour."

"Brother," the cop sighed, "I'm sure glad I caught you before you turned onto Highway 101."

★ ★ ★

The male half of a new dance team was pleading with a producer. "You never saw anything so sensational," the dancer raved. "At the finish of our act, I take my partner by the hair and whirl her around for exactly 20 spins. Then I wind up the whole thing by heaving her through an open window."

"Heave her through an open window?" asked the producer incredulously. "Do you do that at every performance?"

The young dancer shrugged, "Well, no, sometimes I miss."

★ ★ ★

Bill stopped in at Abie's little general store, looking for a bottle of mustard. The shelves were loaded with salt—bags and bags of salt. Abie said he had some mustard, but that he would have to go down to the cellar to find it. Bill went down with him, and there to his surprise were still more bags of salt. Everywhere he looked he could see salt.

"Say," said Bill, "you must sell a lot of salt in this store!"

"Nah," said Abie sourly. "I can't sell no salt. But the feller who sells me salt—boy, can he sell salt!"

★ ★ ★

A driver was busily digging his car out of the mud. A nosy passerby asked him, "Car stuck in the mud?"

The tired driver answered, "Oh, no! My engine just died, and I'm digging a grave for it."

★ ★ ★

Three fellows went into a local restaurant.

"I'd like a tuna sandwich on white bread," said the first fellow.

"Why do you want a tuna sandwich?" asked the waiter. "You must have heard about the mercury problem in tuna. Take a corned beef sandwich. It's more tasty. And besides, why do you want white bread? Take rye bread. It's got more vitamins."

"All right," said the fellow. "Corned beef sandwich on rye bread."

"I'd like some Danish pastry toasted," said the second fellow.

"Why do you want Danish pastry toasted?" asked the waiter. "It just came from the oven. Hot pastry ain't good for you."

"All right," said the second fellow. "Danish pastry plain with a cup of coffee."

"What do you want to take coffee for? It will only keep you awake. Take milk."

"All right," he said. "I'll take Danish pastry plain and a glass of milk."

With that the third fellow asked, "What would you suggest for me?"

"Suggest?" said the waiter. "Who's got time for suggestions?"

★ ★ ★

A man who owned a hand-operated rotisserie was barbecuing a chicken in his backyard when a hippy strolled by. The hippy stood and watched for a couple of minutes and then said slowly, "I don't want to bug you, big daddy, but your music has stopped and your monkey's on fire."

★ ★ ★

A dumb detective was sent out on a murder mystery. The inspector instructed him to go to the house where the murder was committed and to make a thorough search before the inspector got there.

When the inspector arrived he asked the dumb detective if he'd searched the house completely.

"Did you look upstairs, downstairs? Did you look in the closets?" he asked.

"I looked in every closet," replied the detective.

"Did you find any clues?" asked the inspector.

"Yes," replied the detective, "but they didn't fit me."

AT THE GOLF CLUB

A golf foursome was playing on a course where the first three holes parallel a highway. As the foursome trudged down the third fairway, a car drove along the road and stopped abruptly. Out hopped a beautiful girl in full wedding dress. "Henry! Henry!" she sobbed, throwing her arms around one of the players, "Why have you left me waiting at the church?"

"Now, now, Gertrude," he said sternly, "Remember what I said, if it *rained*!"

★ ★ ★

"That's quite a slice you had on that golf ball," the angry cop said to the sheepish duffer. "It curved clear off the course and broke the windshield in my squad car. What do you intend to do about it?"

"Well," replied the golfer. "I was thinking the best thing to do would be to try moving my thumb a little farther up on the club."

★ ★ ★

"Sir, you must be a new member here," said the golf-club member to a golfer. "You should know you can't take your first shot eight feet ahead of the marker."

The golfer ignored the member and continued to address the ball. "Sir," pursued the other, "I must remind you to go back to the marker." The golfer continued to ignore the member.

"Sir, I am chairman of the greens committee and I will have to report you to the board," angrily charged the member.

Finally the golfer looked up and replied, "In the first place, I am not a new member. In the second place, I have been a member of this club for nearly a year and you are the first person who has spoken to me. In the third place, this is my *second* shot!

★ ★ ★

Then there was the golfer who had hit 12 balls into the water on a short waterhole. Suddenly something snapped. He pulled his clubs out of the bag, broke each one, and threw the bag and the golf cart into the water. He stormed into the club house, pulled open his locker, ripped up his golf clothes and set fire to them. Grabbing a razor, he slashed his wrists. An ambulance came, and as he was being carried to it on a stretcher, he noticed in the crowd of shocked spectators one of the members of his foursome. "Sol," he whispered, "what time do we tee off tomorrow?"

One of my friends is called a James Bond golfer. After each hole he picks up the ball and says, "Oh, Oh, Seven!"

★ ★ ★

While playing a short hole, a golfer hit his drive into the rough, where it flushed up a quail. It was, he admitted, the first time he'd seen a partridge on a par three.

★ ★ ★

A Golfing Parody

I think that I shall never see
A hazard rougher than a tree;
A tree o'er which my ball must fly
If on the green it is to lie;
A tree which stands that green to guard,
And makes the shot extremely hard;
A tree whose leafy arms extend
To kill the mashie shot I send;
A tree that stands in silence there,
While angry golfers rave and swear.
Niblicks were made for fools like me
Who cannot ever miss a tree.

HARD TO BELIEVE!

One man walked over to another on the train and greeted him with a slap on the back. "If it isn't my old friend Saltzman! What's happened to you? You used to be so tall—now you're shorter. And you used to be blond—now you've got dark hair. And I remember you had blue eyes—now they're brown."

The man looked at him like he was out of his gourd. "Are you crazy or something? My name is not Saltzman, its Shemmer."

"Oh, my," replied the gent, "you've even changed your name!"

A man went for a ride in an airplane. When he came down he said to the pilot, "Thanks for the two rides."

"Two rides?" asked the aviator. "You've only had one!"

"No," said the gent, "two, my first and my last."

After talking for several hours, the speaker finally ended with, "I'm sorry, my friends, if I have spoken too long—but you see, I don't happen to have a watch with me."

"What's that got to do with it?" shouted one of his victims from the audience. "There's a calendar behind you!"

Customer: "Do you remember that cheese you sold me yesterday?"

Grocer: "Yes, I do. What did you think of it?"

Customer: "Was it imported or deported from Switzerland?"

Freshman: "Well, I went to the football tryouts today."

Girlfriend: "Good! Did you make the team?"

Freshman: "I think so. The coach took one look at me and said, 'This is the end.' "

★ ★ ★

A playboy had been out too late the night before, and in the wrong places. Nursing a magnificent hangover, he stopped in a small all-night catery for breakfast.

"What will you have, sir?" asked the waitress.

"All I want is two fried eggs and a few kind words," replied the bleary-eyed gent. Soon she returned with two pale-looking eggs.

"Here are your eggs, sir," she said, "and now for the kind words—don't eat 'em."

★ ★ ★

The boarder ventured the opinion that the chicken served him was reared in an incubator.

"So it was," the landlady agreed, "but how did you guess it?"

"Well, any chicken that had a mother wouldn't be as tough as this."

★ ★ ★

A man in a restaurant called the waiter over disgustedly. "What do you call this stuff—coffee or tea?" he sneered. "It tastes like kerosene!"

"If it tastes like kerosene," said the waiter calmly, "it must be coffee. The tea tastes like turpentine."

★ ★ ★

Jake, the mail carrier, complained to his boss that a dog had bitten him on the leg that morning. "Did you put anything on it?" asked his boss. "No," replied Jake, "he liked it just as it was."

★ ★ ★

Farmer: "I just bought a new goat."
Friend: "How is he?"
Farmer: "O.K., but he doesn't have a nose."
Friend: "Gosh sakes, How does he smell?"
Farmer: "Simply terrible."

★ ★ ★

Tryouts for the school boxing team were being conducted. Some of the new boxers were good, some not-so-good. One of the latter, after trying hard for a couple of rounds, asked the coach, "Have I done him any damage?"

"No," said the disgusted coach, "but keep on swinging. The draft might give him a cold."

★ ★ ★

A cowboy was bragging about his horse.

"I got the smartest horse you ever saw," he said. "One day while riding I fell off and broke my leg."

"Wait a minute," interrupted another cowboy. "You're not going to tell me he picked you up and put you back in the saddle."

"No, but he dragged me to my bunk, then galloped five miles to get me a doctor. There was only one slip in it. He came back with a horse doctor!"

★ ★ ★

A motorist driving through the Ozarks saw a burly mountaineer wrestling with a big bear—and getting the worst of it. Serenely watching from atop a boulder nearby was the mountaineer's wife, a rifle slung under her arm.

"Quick!" shouted the motorist, "Shoot the beast!"

"Not yet," the wife replied complacently, "I'm a-waitin' to see whether the bear won't save me the trouble."

★ ★ ★

I like the story about the hillbilly who was trying to help his son with his math homework. Neither the kid nor the father was very sharp. "What's two from two?" asked the son of his father. Pappy then explained very carefully, "If I gave you two apples and then took both of them away, how many apples would you have left?"

"That's easy," said the kid. "Nary a one, Paw!"

"That's right, son," the father said. "Put down 'nary'."

★ ★ ★

An enemy spy who had been very effective in his operations was captured. The general gave orders to one of his men to take the spy to a certain area in the woods and have him shot. As they were walking along it began to rain and then to snow. They sloshed through twelve miles of the mushy stuff.

"Isn't it bad enough that you're going to shoot me," said the spy, "without walking me twelve miles yet?"

"What are you squawking about?" said the soldier. "I've got to walk back yet!"

★ ★ ★

The fortune-teller who had collected ten dollars for a short reading informed the anxious teenager, "My fee entitles you to ask me two questions."

"Isn't that a lot of money for only two questions?" the startled teenager asked.

"Yes, it is," agreed the fortune-teller gravely. "And now—what is your second question?"

Chapter 3

HOLY HUMOR

Jake was a regular visitor at the Santa Anita racetrack. One day he noticed an unusual sight. Before the first race, a Catholic priest visited the stable area and went up to one of the horses entered in the first race and gave it a blessing. Jake watched the race very carefully, and sure enough the blessed horse came in first.

Jake followed the priest before the next race, and sure enough he went through a similar procedure again. Jake played a hunch and put some money on the blessed horse. Lo and behold, it came in first and Jake won a nice pot. He continued the same procedure through the rest of the races and won each time.

The biggest race of the day was the last one. Jake decided to put his whole day's winnings on the race for a final killing. He followed the priest at a distance, and sure enough he entered the stable area and visited one of the horses entered in the race. Jake quickly got to the betting windows and put his whole bundle on the horse Come Along.

He went out into the grandstand area, and soon the race was on. Down the stretch came the horses, and as they sped across the finish line, Come Along was so far back you would have to send a telegram to reach him. Jake was crushed. He located the priest and told him what he had been doing. "What happened with your blessing on that last plug? Now I'm cleaned out, thanks to you."

"That's the trouble with you Protestants," sighed the cleric. "You never know the difference between a blessing and the last rites."

A young businessman, a deacon in his local church, was going to New York on business. While he was there he was to purchase a new sign to be hung in front of the church. He copied the motto and dimensions, but when he got to New York he discovered he had left the drawing behind. He wired his wife, "Send motto and dimensions."

An hour later a message came over the wire, and the new clerk, who had just come from lunch and knew nothing of the previous message, read it and fainted. When they looked at the message she had taken, it read: "Unto Us A Child Is Born. 6 feet long and 2 feet wide."

★ ★ ★

Two Nuns were traveling across the state in a station wagon. Due to pure shortsightedness they ran out of gas on a lonely stretch of road. As they stood by their vehicle trying to collect their thoughts, a truck appeared on the horizon. The friendly truck driver saw their plight and stopped to see if he could be of any help. The nuns told him they had been careless and had run out of gas. "I've got plenty of gas," said the truck driver, "but I don't know how to get it from my truck to your wagon without any containers."

Finally one of the sisters got an inspiration and returned with a bedpan which happened to be in the wagon. "This will be fine," said the driver; "I can fill this from my tanks and it should be enough to get you to the Shell station which is just a mile down the road."

He filled the bedpan and gave it to the women. They thanked him profusely, and he returned to his truck to complete his trip. The sisters were pouring the gasoline from the bedpan into their station wagon's tank when two traveling salesmen happened by in their sedan. They saw the amazing sight as they passed by, and one of them said to the other, "Now that's what I call real faith!"

★ ★ ★

The hotel clerk was shocked to see a guest parading through the foyer in a pair of pajamas.

"Hey, what are you doing?" he asked.

The guest snapped out of it and apologized, "I beg your pardon. I'm a somnambulist."

"Well," sneered the clerk, "you can't walk around here like that, no matter what your religion is."

★ ★ ★

After the collection hat was passed, the pastor saw that it was empty when it was returned.

Slowly and deliberately, the parson inverted the hat and shook it meaningfully. Then, raising his eyes to heaven, he exclaimed fervently, "I thank Thee, Dear Lord, that I got my hat back from this congregation!"

★ ★ ★

Preacher: "How come I never see you in church anymore, Morris?"

Morris: "There are too many hypocrites there, Reverent!"

Preacher: "Don't worry, fellow; there's always room for one more."

★ ★ ★

Minister: "I hope you won't charge too much to fix my car. I'm a poor preacher."

Mechanic: "Yes, I know. I heard you last Sunday."

The minister took seven putts upon one green,
And uttered not a word profane;
But where he spat, ere exiting the scene
No blade of grass will ever grow again.

★ ★ ★

A minister dropped into a strange barber shop for a quick shave and had the sad misfortune to choose a chair presided over by a barber who was suffering from an acute hangover. His breath nearly asphyxiated the poor minister, and then, to cap the climax, he took a huge nick out of the minister's chin. "You see," said the minister reproachfully, "what comes from drinking intoxicating liquor?"

"Yep, sure do," agreed the barber cheerfully. "It makes the skin mighty tender."

★ ★ ★

The new minister was pleased to hear his housekeeper singing "When the Roll Is Called up Yonder" in the kitchen as she prepared breakfast.

"I'm delighted," he told her when she served his breakfast, "that you are such a religious person, Mrs. Jones. I heard you singing my favorite hymn as you were cooking."

"Oh, that," replied Mrs. Jones with a chuckle: "It's what I boil eggs by. Three verses for soft and five for hard."

★ ★ ★

Jimmy and Bill, aged six and ten, were spending a week with their grandmother while their parents were away from home on a visit.

It was a few nights before Christmas, and the kids were getting ready for bed. Their grandmother was in an adjoining room waiting for them to retire so she could turn out the light.

Jimmy said his prayers and crawled under the covers. Bill, still on his knees, proceeded to petition heaven for a long list of Christmas presents. As he progressed his voice rose louder and louder, and he began to repeat himself.

Annoyed, Jimmy got up and protested, "Say, you don't have to pray so loud; the Lord ain't deaf!"

"I know He ain't," said Bill, "but Grandma is."

★ ★ ★

The young rural minister was visiting in one of his parishoner's homes, enjoying a cup of coffee and some small talk. Suddenly the ten-year-old son burst through the back door carrying a big rat by the tail. "Don't worry, Mom," he reassured her, "he's dead. First I clobbered him, then I hit him with a two-by-four, and then I kicked him, then I stamped on him and then I—" At this moment he spotted the minister and concluded in a subdued voice, "and then the Good Lord took his soul to heaven."

★ ★ ★

The devil challenged St. Peter to a baseball game. "How can you win, Satan?" asked St. Peter. "All the famous ballplayers are up here." "How can I lose?" answered Satan. "All the umpires are down here."

★ ★ ★

A rabbi and a Catholic Priest were discussing the future of the younger generation. The priest told how his nephew was attending a theological seminary so that he might become a clergyman. The rabbi asked the priest what careers would be open to the young student. "Well," replied the priest, "he might become a priest or he might choose to become a chaplain in the armed forces.

"What after that?" asked the rabbi.

"Well, he could become a cardinal in time," answered the priest.

"And then?" pursued the rabbi.

"Well, he might even become the Pope someday."

"And then?" asked the rabbi again.

"And then?" repeated the priest in amazement. "What more do you want? Do you imagine that he could become God?"

"Well," replied the rabbi softly, "one of our boys made it."

Chapter 4

POETRY?

They reached the gate in silence,
  He lifted down the bars;
They walked the lane together
  The sky was covered with stars.

She raised her brown eyes to him,
  There's nothing between them now,
For he was just a farmer's son,
  And she a Jersey cow.

★ ★ ★

This is the story of Johnnie McGuire,
Who ran through the town with his pants on fire.
He went to the doctor and fainted with fright,
When the doctor told him his end was in sight.

★ ★ ★

Here's the story of little Nell,
Who fell headfirst into a well.
Mother said while drawing water,
"My, it's hard to raise a daughter!"

★ ★ ★

Before I heard the doctors tell
  The dangers of a kiss,
I had considered kissing you
  The nearest thing to bliss.

But now I know biology
  And sit and sigh and moan;
Six million mad bacteria,
  And I thought we were alone.

★ ★ ★

Dinner's defrosting,
Mother's not;
Today's her birthday,
And Dad forgot.

★ ★ ★

"Boys, I've quit the holdup game—
  I'll hang around the joints no more."
Limp and worn, threadbare and torn,
  The garter fell to the floor.

LIMERICK LANE

There was a young man of Peru
Who dreamed he was eating a shoe.
  He woke up at night
  With a terrible fright
And found it was perfectly true.

★ ★ ★

There was a young man named Burkey
Who could not tell chickens from turkey.
  Both Latin and Greek
  He could fluently speak,
But his knowledge of poultry was murky.

★ ★ ★

There was a young man from the city
Who met what he thought was a kitty.
  He gave it a pat,
  And said, "Nice little cat,"
So they buried his clothes out of pity.

★ ★ ★

There once was a young lady named Tess
Whose necking was rather a mess.
  But in less than a week
  She acquired a technique,
And now she's a social success.

★ ★ ★

There were two cats in Kilkenny;
Each thought there was one cat too many.
  So they scratched and they spit,
  And they tore and they bit,
And instead of two cats there aren't any.

★ ★ ★

A dashing young fellow named Tim
Drove his car with a great deal of vim;
  Said he, "I'm renowned
  For covering ground,"
But, alas, now the ground covers him.

MISCELLANY

Don't like the teacher,
The subject's too deep;
I'd cut the class
But I need the sleep.

There are things in life
That modern man keeps groping for—
Faith, hope, and love,
And the light switch by the door.

★ ★ ★

There was a young pastor in Kew
Who kept a brown cow in a pew.
There he taught it each week
A new letter in Greek,
But it never got farther than MU.

★ ★ ★

It is easy enough to be happy
When life is a bright, rosy wreath.
But the man worthwhile
Is the man who can smile
When the dentist is filling his teeth.

★ ★ ★

Down the street his funeral goes,
As sobs and wails diminish;
He died from drinking straight shellac,
But he had a lovely finish.

★ ★ ★

Here's to the stork,
A most valuable bird
That inhabits the residential districts.
He doesn't sing tunes
Nor yield any plumes,
But he helps out the vital statistics.

★ ★ ★

Daddy bought a little car
And feeds it gasoline,
And everywhere that Daddy goes
He walks—his son's sixteen.

★ ★ ★

Her cookie jar is always filled,
Her car is at the ready;
She never shouts when milk is spilled,
She lets her kids go steady.

She rings a most indulgent curfew,
Her cooking's like no other.
Who is this paragon of virtue?
Why, *everybody else's* mother!

★ ★ ★

If you your lips would save from slips,
Five things observe with care:
Of whom you speak, to whom you speak,
And how, and when, and where.

★ ★ ★

I never see my preacher's eyes,
He hides their light divine.
For when he prays he shuts his own,
And when he preaches, mine.

★ ★ ★

Two starry-eyed, reckless young beaux
Were held up and robbed of their cleaux.
While the weather is hot
They won't miss them a lot,
But what will they do when it sneaux?

From way down in my cranium
I this prediction make:
If you eat uranium
You'll get atomic ache.

I did my best to show him how,
To hold his lips just so;
I told him to be ready
When I gave the signal *Go*!
He puckered up and closed his eyes
And did as he was told.
It's hard to learn to whistle
When you're only three years old!

He climbed up the door
And shut the stairs;
He said his shoes
And took off his prayers.
He shut off the bed
And climbed into the light;
And all because
She kissed him goodnight.

"O bury me not on the lone prairie,"
The dying cowboy said;
"The sun is much too hot out here,
And besides that, I ain't dead."

Bather, bather, burning bright,
Seeking for new sides to fry on,
How you're gonna wish tonight
You had saved a side to lie on!

Chapter 5

PUNNY BUT FUNNY

Two Spanish detectives were standing over the body of Juan Gonzalez. "How was he shot?" inquired the first.

"I theenk eet was a golf gun," said the other.

"But what ees a golf gun?" asked his buddy.

"Who knows," came back the reply, "but eet sure made a hole in Juan."

★ ★ ★

There was a news story of a young U.S. Navy petty officer who gained his discharge from the service. He had served valiantly, and, being a full-blooded Indian, he returned to his reservation to help less fortunate members of his tribe. Anxious to freshen up for the dinner planned to welcome him, he paid his first visit to the head, only to find it shrouded in darkness. So he promptly had the head electrified at his own expense—the first time in history anybody wired a head for a reservation.

★ ★ ★

He: What do you get when you cross a movie house with a swimming pool?

She: A dive-in theater.

★ ★ ★

Jeb was 75 and Minnie was 73. They had met at a senior citizens' gathering, and love had blossomed into marriage. The doctor examined them before their marriage, and when he asked why they wanted to get married, it seemed they both had some money and they wanted to have an heir. The doctor looked at them both and said gravely, "There's no reason why you shouldn't get married, but I think you're both more heir-minded than you are heir-conditioned."

DID YOU HEAR ABOUT . . .

. . . the intrepid hunter in the lush jungles of Ceylon who was so intent upon bagging a treacherous leopard that, in the excitement, his false teeth fell out? Ever since the poor man has been searching for his bridge on the River Kwai.

★ ★ ★

. . . the short-tempered father? He yelled to his son, "If you fall off that rock and break your leg, don't come running to me!"

★ ★ ★

. . . the undertaker who married a snake charmer? They had towels marked "Hiss" and "Hearse."

★ ★ ★

. . . the farmer? He called his rooster "Robinson" because he crew so.

★ ★ ★

. . . the farmer in Wisconsin had a son who went to New York City and became a bootblack? Now the farmer makes hay while the son shines.

. . . the French? They're trying to buy the Rock of Gibraltar from the British. They want to make a monument out of it in honor of their late great Premier—They want to name it "De Gaulle Stone."

. . . the father of four sets of twins? He sued for divorce on the grounds that his wife was over-bearing.

TWOSOMES

Oscar: "I have an uncle who's conceited. He's six-foot-six and plays the flute."

Bill: "What makes you think he's conceited just because he's six-foot-six and plays the flute?"

Oscar: "Well, that's high-flutin', isn't it?"

Moe: "Say, Joe, how did you get that swelling on your nose?"

Joe: "I was bending down to smell a brose in my garden."

Moe: "Silly oaf. There's no B in rose."

Joe: "There was in this one!"

He: "What do you think of a 42-year-old woman who sleeps with cats?"

She: "Who in the world does that?"

He: "Mrs. Katz!"

★ ★ ★

He: What kind of corsage did Lassie wear to the big ball of the year?

She: Probably a collie flower.

He: What do you get when you cross an elephant with a mosquito?

She: I don't know. What?

He: A forget-me-gnat.

COME AGAIN?

A grandmother sent her grandson a shirt for Christmas. The only trouble was that he had a size 16 neck, and the shirt was size 14. The grandson wrote a thank-you note and said, "Dear Grandma: Thanks a lot for the shirt. I'd write more but I'm all choked up."

The circus manager told the human cannonball, "You can't quit now! Where can I find another man of your caliber?"

You could never get Max Steinbaum to go on any kind of a hike. He was known in his high school yearbook as "Anti-climb Max."

And then there's the dentist who married the manicurist, and they've been fighting tooth and nail ever since.

A diet is something that takes the starch out of you.

Did you hear about the girl with the Supreme Court figure? No appeal.

MORE TWOSOMES

"Oh, Doctor, I'm so worried. My baby swallowed the film from my camera."

"There is no cause for worry, Madam. I don't believe anything will develop."

"I can't make up my mind whether to be a psychiatrist or an author."

"Why not toss for it—heads or tales?"

"Doc, my wife gets very historical when I stay out nights."

"You mean hysterical, don't you?"

"No, I mean historical. She digs up the past."

"How is that sailor who swallowed the half-dollar?"

"No change yet, sir."

He: What do you call a Hong Kong girl who inherits ten million yen?

She: A Chinese fortunate cookie.

★ ★ ★

Mary: "I ran into Lois today. I hadn't seen her in years."

Lynn: "Oh, has she kept her girlish figure?"

Mary: "Kept it! She's doubled it!"

THREE IN A ROW

A prominent doctor has discovered that cheerful people resist disease better than chronic grumblers. His theory is that the surly bird catches the germ.

★ ★ ★

There are some people you just don't like to be around very much. Everytime you're with them they start telling you all the great things they've accomplished. As one fellow said, "Everytime they open their mouths they put their feats in them."

★ ★ ★

A California sucker bought some Oregon land sight unseen. When he went to visit his paradise he discovered the land was 90% swampland, infested by bugs and vermin. When he checked with his lawyer, the attorney read the deed and said, "Sorry, old chap, but I'm afraid they've left you holding the bog!"

TWOSOMES AGAIN

He: What's the best way to clean an aardvark?
She: With an aardvarkuum-cleaner.

★ ★ ★

Tony: How was spaghetti invented?
Mike: A good Italian simply used his noodle.

★ ★ ★

Pat: What did one IBM card say to the other card?
Mike: I'm holier than thou.

Angie: "The Sing Sing Prison football team played West Point last week."
Frank: "How'd they come out?"
Angie: "Sing Sing won 12 to 7, thus proving that the pen is mightier than the sword."

Sherlock: "If a man smashed a clock, could he be accused of killing time?"
Watson: "Not if he could prove that the clock struck first."

Mechanic: "Lady, I've found the trouble with your car. You've got a short circuit in the wiring."
Lady: "Well, for heaven's sake, lengthen it!"

Wilmer: "I sure wish you would stop reaching for things. Don't you have a tongue?"
Delbert: "Yeah, but my arm is longer."

Will: "What's your average income?"
Fred: "Oh, about midnight."

Florrie: "But surely you didn't tell him straight out that you loved him?"
Dorrie: "Goodness, no—he had to squeeze it out of me."

PROVERBS WITH A TWIST

Be it ever so homely, there's no face like your own.

★ ★ ★

Be true to thy teeth, and they will not be false to thee.

★ ★ ★

A good line is the shortest distance between two dates.

★ ★ ★

Everything comes to him who orders hash.

★ ★ ★

Time, tide, and women drivers wait for no man.

★ ★ ★

Hair today—gone tomorrow.

★ ★ ★

Absence makes the heart go wander.

★ ★ ★

As it snows, so shall ye sweep.

★ ★ ★

As ye smoke, so shall ye reek.

Money can be lost in more ways than won.

★ ★ ★

Eat, drink, and be merry, for tomorrow we diet.

★ ★ ★

One good turn gets most of the blanket.

★ ★ ★

Great aches from little toe-corns grow.

STILL PUNNY

Pedro suffered from insomnia, but then he fell in love with a Mexican beauty named Esta. Now when he wants to sleep, he just looks at her picture. Pedro knew from childhood that when you see Esta, you sleep.

★ ★ ★

A barber named Cohen had a shop located next to a bowling alley. He was determined to improve his score, so he began spending more and more time in the alley, neglecting his own shop. He had made three successive strikes one afternoon when the political boss of the county tracked him down and demanded an immediate shave. But Cohen pushed him aside indignantly, declaring firmly, "A bowling Cohen lathers no boss!"

★ ★ ★

A very beautiful girl had a knee which was completely out of joint. She visited a chiropractor in search of some help. The doctor examined her with relish and rose to inquire, "What's a joint like this doing in a pretty girl like you?"

All afternoon a real estate agent had been showing a young couple empty houses. The ones they hated always seemed to be available, but the ones they liked had always been snapped up by other people. Finally they came to a house at the very edge of town, and they fell in love with it. "Please," they begged, "tell us we can have this one."

"It's yours," beamed the agent. "It's last but not leased!"

WHAT! MORE TWOSOMES?

Jake: "Do you call this art? This drawing looks amateurish."

Pablo: "Well, it's a matter of sketch as sketch can."

★ ★ ★

Cop: "Hey, don't you see that sign that says 'Fine for Parking'?"

Lady Driver: "Yes, officer, I see it, and I heartily agree with it."

★ ★ ★

Tom: "Boy, did we throw a big party in our cellar last night!"

Joan: "You don't say! Was your Uncle Willie there?"

Tom: "Was he! He was the big party we threw in the cellar!"

Herb: "I should have been a songwriter—I have a squeaking shoe."

Mary: "What has a squeaking shoe got to do with being a songwriter?"

Herb: "I've got music in my sole!"

★ ★ ★

Manny: "Do you file your nails?"

Jane: "No, silly, I just cut them off and throw them away."

★ ★ ★

Freshman: "I'm majoring in ancient history."

Co-ed: "So am I."

Freshman: "Great! We'll have to get together and talk over old times."

PUNNIER THAN EVER

Scientists are still experimenting with methods of making milk. No matter how they do it, I still prefer the udder way.

★ ★ ★

Medical authorities say that singing warms the blood. That is an actual fact, for I've heard some singing that makes my blood boil.

★ ★ ★

Mama flea looked worried. When papa flea asked why the sadness, she replied, "All our children are going to the dogs."

Did you hear about the cannibal who ate his nagging mother-in-law, then found she still disagreed with him?

One woman mixed her birth control pills with Saccharin. She now has the sweetest baby around.

Give dandelions an inch and they'll take a yard.

She'd be more spick if she had less span.

She's been dieting, waiting for hips that never come in.

She was only the village belle, but she should have been tolled.

Coffee break: the time of day when the company lets the business go to pot.

Old maids are girls who talk about boy-gone days.

I was born a blonde and I'll dye a blonde.

She was suffering from a severe case of he-fever.

★ ★ ★

They had several children in rabbit succession.

★ ★ ★

Babysitters fulfill an important job. They meet a crying need.

★ ★ ★

With acupuncture becoming so popular, there may soon be a Mao Clinic.

★ ★ ★

The paratroopers were being instructed on the use of their chutes.

"What if it doesn't open?" asked one rookie.

"That, my friend," said the instructor, "is known as jumping to a conclusion!"

Chapter 6

LOVE AND MARRIAGE

The after-dinner speaker was handed a note just before he was due to speak. It was from his wife and said simply, "KISS, Betty." The lady sitting next to him remarked, "How sweet of your wife to remind you of her love just before you have to make an important speech."

"That isn't quite the message," he explained. "What this note means is 'Keep It Short, Stupid!' "

★ ★ ★

An incorrigible old reprobate of 86 years consulted his doctor before taking to himself a naive bride of 21. "Marry her if you must," said the doctor dubiously, "but restrain yourself. Overexertion could well prove fatal."

The reprobate shrugged his shoulders and philosophised, "Well, if she dies, she dies."

★ ★ ★

The woman lecturer was going strong. "For thousands of years women have been maligned and mistreated," she thundered. "They have suffered in a million ways. Is there any way that women have not suffered?"

As she paused to let that question sink in, a quiet masculine voice answered: "Yes! They have never suffered in silence!"

Jones was sitting with his wife behind a palm on a hotel veranda late one night when a young man and girl came and sat down on a bench near them. Hidden behind the palm, Mrs. Jones whispered to her husband, "Oh, John, he doesn't know we're here and he's going to propose to her. Whistle to warn him."

"What for?" said Jones, "Nobody whistled to warn me."

★ ★ ★

A girl, about to be married, received a present of a silk dress from her mother.

"How do you like it?" asked the mother.

"Oh, Mother," said the girl, "it's just beautiful."

"That's for you to be married in," said the mother.

The girl kept looking at the dress. She seemed rather serious.

"What are you thinking of, Honey?" asked the mother.

"I was just thinking," commented the girl "I should be grateful to the poor little worm for this silk dress."

"Just a minute, my dear," scolded her mother. "Don't talk like that about your father."

★ ★ ★

Asked one gal of another at a dinner party, "Doesn't it embarrass you to see your husband flirting so shamelessly with all the younger women?"

"Oh, I just let him have his innocent pleasure," said the wife tolerantly. "He's really very harmless. He's like a puppy chasing automobiles. He wouldn't know what to do if he caught one. He just wants to bark at them a little."

★ ★ ★

When children reach a certain age they begin to get curious about what brought their parents together. All day a wife crabbed freely at her husband, but in the evening the two of them were sitting in the backyard when their six-year-old son asked, "Daddy, how did you meet Mother?"

Growled father, "I took a thorn out of her paw."

LOVE-AND-MARRIAGE TWOSOMES

He: "I dreamed I was married to the most beautiful girl in the world."

She: "Isn't that exciting. Were we happy?"

★ ★ ★

She: "Do you really love me, Dear?"

He: "You know I do, Sweetheart!"

She: "Would you die for me?"

He: "Of course not, my pet. Mine is an undying love."

★ ★ ★

Jake: "Didn't the kiss I just gave you make you long for another?"

Mary: "Sure, but he's away on a trip this week."

★ ★ ★

"Doesn't the bride look stunning?"

"Yes, and doesn't the groom look stunned?"

★ ★ ★

Young wife: "Don't forget to bring home another mousetrap."

Husband: "What's the matter with the one I brought yesterday?"

Young wife: "It's full."

★ ★ ★

Traffic cop: "I'm afraid your wife fell out of your car about a mile back."

Driver: "Thank goodness! I thought I'd gone deaf."

★ ★ ★

He: "You don't deserve a husband like me."

She: "I don't deserve sinus trouble either, but I have it."

THIS IS LOVE?

The wife had spent the whole afternoon trying to balance her checkbook. When her husband came home, she handed him four neatly typed sheets, with items and costs in their respective columns. He read them over carefully.

Milkman, $3.25, cleaners, $4.75, phone bill $11.20, etc. Everything was clear except one item reading ESP, $24.49.

Warily, he asked her, "What does ESP mean?"
"Error some place," she explained.

★ ★ ★

The tiny little wife dragged her drinking husband into court and demanded a divorce instantly. Trying to pacify her, the judge asked her if her husband had ever tried Alcoholics Anonymous.

The frail woman dabbed at her eyes and said, "I guess so, Your Honor. He'll drink anything."

In the ten years they had been married, Mrs. Swartz had presented her husband with 12 splendid children. One day Mr. Schwartz warned his wife: "You've got to stop this, Honey—it's getting so that when I come home from work, I'm afraid to ask what's new!"

People are funny. I know a guy who didn't kiss his wife for ten years—then he goes and shoots a fellow who did.

What an evening gown. You couldn't tell whether she was inside trying to get out, or outside trying to get in.

An old maid left a ten-dollar bill on the bureau. A burglar came in, grabbed the bill, kissed her and beat it. The next night she put a twenty-dollar bill there.

LOVE-AND-MARRIAGE QUICKIES

Have you read about those new gadgets that can tell when a man is lying?

Read about them? I married one.

I'll never forget the first time I put my arm around my bride-to-be. Right away I felt a lump in my throat. She was a karate expert.

She knows her Darwin backwards—she can make a monkey out of any man.

My wife and I had words—but I never got a chance to use mine.

He told her he wanted some old-fashioned loving, so she introduced him to her grandmother.

He may be old but he's still in there pinching.

Confucius say, "Wash face in the morning—neck at night."

If a fellow and girl spend seven evenings a week in each other's company, and both think it would be so much nicer if they could be together all the time—that's love.

Studying English sure didn't help him very much. He still ends all his sentences with a proposition.

An angry lady demanding a divorce gave as her reason that her husband had insisted on washing her face. "What's wrong with that?" asked the judge; "cleanliness is next to godliness."

"You didn't let me finish," continued the wife; "then he ironed it!"

I've been married 32 years and I don't regret one day of it. The one day I don't regret was June 10, 1944!

I've had 18 happy married years. Eighteen out of 26 isn't a bad average!

"I'm truly distressed that my wife should be bothering you with her imaginary troubles," a husband told a marriage counselor. "The only complaint what's-her-name keeps accusing me of is that I don't pay enough attention to her."

Adam and Eve had an ideal marriage. He didn't have to hear about all the men she could have married — and she didn't have to hear about the way his mother cooked it.

He kept whispering sweet nothings in her ear and she kept whispering back sweet nothing-doings.

I saw this gal down in Miami Beach—I wouldn't say her bathing suit was skimpy, but I've seen more cotton on top of an aspirin bottle.

HOW TRUE, HOW TRUE!

Marrying a modern girl is a liberal education in itself. Before marriage she knows all the answers, and after marriage she knows all the questions.

Marrying a woman for her beauty is like buying a house for its paint.

Lovemaking hasn't changed much in 2500 years. Greek girls used to sit and listen to a Lyre all evening too.

People used to marry for better or worse. Now it's for more or less.

When Cupid hits the mark he usually Mrs. it.

A man picks a wife the same way an apple picks a farmer.

Love is like a bazaar. The admission is free, but it costs you something before you get out.

A man never falls in love with a woman he understands, but with the woman who understands him.

★ ★ ★

What is the bride thinking about as the organ plays the wedding march? "Aisle—Altar—Hymn."

★ ★ ★

Marriage is a hit-or-miss proposition—if you don't make a hit you remain a miss.

★ ★ ★

Before marriage a girl has to kiss a man to hold him; after marriage she has to hold him to kiss him.

★ ★ ★

Never tell a woman you are unworthy of her. Let her find out for herself.

YOU'LL LOVE THESE!

A lawyer complained to the marriage counselor that the reason his marriage was going on the rocks was because his wife was so immature. "Would you believe it? Everytime I take a bath she comes in and sinks all my boats!"

★ ★ ★

A marriage counselor was asking a woman some questions about her disposition.

"Did you wake up grumpy this morning?" he asked.

"No," replied the woman, "I just let him sleep."

An irate lady, seeking a divorce in court, told the judge, "My husband is an out-and-out loafer who thinks about nothing day and night except horse-racing. He doesn't even remember our wedding day."

"That's a lie!" shouted the outraged husband. "We were married the day Twenty Grand won the Kentucky Derby."

★ ★ ★

"You won't catch me getting hitched," maintained a confirmed bachelor, "until I discover a girl just like the girl who married dear old Granddad." "Forget it," chided a friend. "They don't make girls like that anymore." "The heck you say," chuckled the bachelor. "Granddad married this one a week ago last Tuesday."

★ ★ ★

Her lips quivered as they approached his. His whole frame trembled as he looked into her eyes. Her chin vibrated and his body shuddered as he held her close to him.

MORAL: Never kiss a girl in a jeep with the motor running.

Chapter 7

HERE'S TO YOUR HEALTH

A woman's husband suddenly became violently ill, so she called up Dr. Smith to come right over. He arrived with his doctor's satchel and told her to wait outside the sickroom while he went in and examined her husband. After half an hour he rushed out and yelled, "I've got to have a chisel right away."

The wife got frightened and froze, and the doctor shouted again, "If you can't get me a chisel, get me a hammer or a screwdriver. Quick!"

She couldn't find anything, so she ran next door to her neighbor's and returned with a hammer, a chisel, and a screwdriver.

"Here they are, Doctor. I hope it's nothing serious. Am I too late? What's the matter with my husband?"

"I can't tell yet," replied the doctor. "I can't get my satchel open."

★ ★ ★

The doctor said, "The best thing for you to do is to give up drinking and smoking, get up early every morning, and go to bed early every night."

The patient replied, "Doctor, I don't deserve the best. What's second best?"

★ ★ ★

Mrs. Bunning complained so bitterly about her aches and pains that her husband reluctantly sent for the doctor, who eventually arrived and jammed a thermometer into her mouth.

"Keep absolutely quiet for five minutes," warned the doctor—and Mrs. Bunning obeyed meekly.

"Doctor," asked the longsuffering Mr. Bunning, "what will you take for that thing?"

★ ★ ★

A woman who had driven the other members of a first-aid class nearly frantic by her continued criticism of the whole idea turned up one morning a complete convert—first-aid training was a wonderful thing, it ought to be compulsory.

"Why," she said, "yesterday I was sitting at home when I heard a screeching of brakes and then a terrific crash. Two cars had turned over right in front of our gate, and four people were lying in the street. One woman had a deep cut in her arm, two men had broken legs, and another had severe lacerations of the face. But, thank heaven, I remembered exactly what you taught me. So I bent over and put my head between my knees—and I didn't even faint!"

★ ★ ★

The guest was ready to deliver his speech at a formal banquet when he discovered that his upper plate was cracked. "You'll have to cancel my speech," he whispered to the M.C., and he proceeded to explain his dilemma.

"Nonsense," said the M.C., "here's a spare upper I have in my coat pocket." The guest of honor inserted the plate in his mouth and tried a few words, but with disastrous results. "No good," he told the M.C.; "they don't fit."

Like a magician taking rabbits out of a hat, the M.C. produced a second plate, which didn't fit either, and then a third plate, which was exactly right.

The guest of honor made a fine speech, received an ovation, then turned gratefully to the M.C. and said, "It was a lucky break for me that you happen to be a dentist."

"Dentist, nothing," said the M.C. "I'm an undertaker."

★ ★ ★

"You've got to straighten out my husband," pleaded a wife to a Hollywood psychiatrist. "He thinks he's a jet plane."

"Bring him here Thursday at two," suggested the psychiatrist. "I will need to examine him and then start remedial steps."

"Oh, I can't do that, Doctor," said the wife. "He's got to appear in court that afternoon for flying low over Glendale."

★ ★ ★

"Now," said the head doctor to his new patient, "we're going to find out just what makes you tick."

"That won't be enough," mourned the patient. "I also want to know what makes me chime every quarter of an hour."

★ ★ ★

A clumsy fool swallowed a ping pong ball during a crucial match. He was rushed to a local hospital to have it removed. He was calm and brave while the surgeon made an incision, but began to squirm when this was followed by two more painful jabs. When the surgeon prepared to make a fourth probing cut, the patient exclaimed, "What's the big idea of cutting me in so many places?"

"Relax, man," suggested the doctor. "That's the way the ball bounces."

"Come, come," the smiling psychiatrist said to his sobbing patient. "you mustn't carry on like this. Cheer up! Be happy!"

"Be happy!" echoed the tearful woman. "How can I be happy? Sixteen children I've had by that no-good husband of mine, and he doesn't even love me. What is there for me to be happy about?"

"Well," suggested the doctor, "imagine what it would have been like if he did love you."

★ ★ ★

"I want a tooth pulled," the man said to the dentist when he entered the office with his wife, "and we're in a hurry, so let's not fool around with gas or Novacaine or any of that jazz."

"Say," said the dentist, "you're a real brave man. Which tooth is it?"

"Show him your bad tooth, Ethel," said the man to his wife.

★ ★ ★

To the most famous and expensive doctor in the area came a gent who admitted at the outset that he couldn't afford the $500 fee. In a good mood, the doctor reduced the tab to $400. "But, Doc," pleaded the man, "I have a wife and five kids to support." The fee was lowered to $250.

"For me that's a month's rent," sighed the man—and it was in this way that the fee went down to $100 and finally to $30.

"I'm the top specialist in my field," the doctor remonstrated, "and admittedly the highest priced. Why did you come to me anyhow?"

"Because," asserted the man vehemently, "when my health is involved, money is no object!"

★ ★ ★

A country doctor had occasion to phone the town's only drugstore in the middle of a hot midsummer afternoon. "Hello," drawled a lazy voice after ten rings of the phone. "Now listen carefully," ordered the doctor. "I need these two prescriptions filled right away." He then rattled off the names of several ingredients, some in five syllables. When he was finished he demanded, "Have you got all that straight?"

The lazy voice answered patiently, "Mister, when I said Hello I done exhausted my vocabulary."

★ ★ ★

The psychiatrist told the husband of one of his patients, "I'm sorry to have to tell you this, but your wife's mind is gone."

"I'm not surprised," replied the husband. "She's been giving me a piece of it every day."

★ ★ ★

An asylum attendant rushed over to the doctor. "There's a man outside who wants to know if we've lost any male inmates!"

"Why?" asked the medical man.

"He says someone ran away with his wife."

★ ★ ★

"Doctor! Doctor!" screamed the young mother. "My young son just swallowed a .45 caliber bullet!"

"O.K., calm down, lady," counseled the doctor. "Give him two tablespoons of castor oil before putting him to bed, and in the meantime don't point him at anybody!"

Tom: "I'm worried about my cousin. He thinks he's an elevator."

Doctor: "Well, I'll look at him. Send him up."

Tom: "I can't. He doesn't stop at your floor."

★ ★ ★

Psychiatrist: "I wouldn't worry about your son making mudpies. It's quite normal."

Mother: "Well, I don't think so and neither does his wife!"

★ ★ ★

My doctor got me on my feet in no time. I had to sell the car to pay his bill.

★ ★ ★

Patient: "Fifty dollars seems like a lot of money for pulling a tooth. It only takes about 30 seconds of work."

Dentist: "Well, if it will make you feel any better, I can pull it very slowly."

★ ★ ★

A surgeon was completing his two thousandth successful operation. Another doctor walked in and asked, "How did you accomplish such a remarkable feat?" The surgeon replied, "It took a lot of patients!"

★ ★ ★

An extremely distraught man entered the office of a psychiatrist. "Doctor," he began his session, "I can't seem to remember anything from one minute to the next."

"Since when has this been going on?" asked the psychiatrist.

"Since when has what been going on?" retorted the gent.

★ ★ ★

The dentist had a nervous patient in his chair and was trying to extract a bad tooth, but everytime he got ready to proceed, the patient clamped his jaws shut.

At last the dentist took his assistant aside and told her that, at the very moment he poised the forceps, she should give the patient's hip a vicious pinch.

The pinch was administered, the nervous patient's mouth flew open, and the tooth was quickly extracted.

"There," said the dentist, "that didn't hurt too much, did it?" "Not much," replied the patient, "but who would have thought the roots went that deep?"

★ ★ ★

A fellow smashed his fingers and went to a doctor for treatment. After he was fixed up he asked the doctor, "Say, Doc, will I be able to play the piano when these fingers heal?"

"You certainly will," replied the doctor assuredly.

"Gee, thanks, Doc, you're a marvel," replied the chap. "I never could play the piano before."

Chapter 8

ALL AROUND THE WORLD

Three Jewish boys had really made it big as a banker, a stockbroker, and an industrialist. Their widowed mother was proud of them, and when she neared her eightieth birthday each of her sons wanted to do something special for her. Unfortunately, they were all extremely busy, so they arranged to have the gifts sent to her ahead of time. Hymie, the banker, ordered a beautiful mink coat for $3,000 and had it sent by parcel post. Abie, the stockbroker, pulled out all the stops and ordered a brand new blue Cadillac which set him back a cool $12,000, but it was worth it. It was delivered right on time.

Morey wanted to do something real special, and, knowing how lonesome his mother got, he ordered a special rare bird that could speak just like a human being. It cost him a mere $15,000, but nothing was too good for his dear mother.

Her birthday arrived, and the fellows managed to clear their calendars and converge on the old homestead to enjoy this happy occasion with Mama. Hymie arrived first and asked Mama how she liked her new coat. "Oh," she said, "Hymie, I just love it. It keeps me so nice and warm and I wear it everywhere. I just hate to take it off at night." "That's good, Mama," said Hymie with delight in his voice.

Abie came next, and after proper greetings were exchanged he asked Mama how she liked her new car. "Oh," she exclaimed with delight, "I just love it. It takes me everywhere I want to go. The neighbors are so jealous of me. You couldn't have done anything better for me." Abie was pleased.

Morey of course was next, and He was curious to see just how much Mama had enjoyed his $15,000 talking bird. "Mama," asked Morey with anticipation, "how did you like the nice bird I sent you?" "Oh," Mama replied, "it was delicious."

SCOTTIES

A Scotsman planning a trip to the Holy Land was aghast when he found it would cost the equivalent of ten shillings an hour to rent a boat on the Sea of Galilee. "Mon," he said indignantly, "anywhere in Scotland it would be a lot cheaper."

"Perhaps so," said the travel agent soothingly, "but remember, the Sea of Galilee is the water on which our Lord walked."

The Scotsman shook his head sadly. "It's nae wonder He walked!"

★ ★ ★

Wandering aimlessly on a lonely road in Scotland, an American at last met up with another human—a kilted highlander.

"Gosh, pal," remarked the American, "I'm lost."

"Is there a reward out for ye?" inquired the Scot.

"Why, no."

"Weel," remarked the Scotsman, walking on, "ye're still lost."

★ ★ ★

"A penny for your thoughts," said Sandy's girlfriend to him one day.

"Wel-l-l, I was thinking I'd like to kiss ye, Lassie," replied the Scotsman. The kiss was lovely, and a minute later Sandy was in deep thought again.

"And what are ye thinkin' noo, Sandy, another kiss, perhaps?" said she.

"No, lassie," Sandy gravely responded. "I was just wonderin' when ye were goin' to pay me that penny for my thoughts."

★ ★ ★

Up in Minnesota a railroad train killed a cow belonging to a Swedish homesteader. The tragedy was reported at headquarters, and a claim agent was sent to the spot to make a settlement of damages.

The claim agent was a persuasive person, so when he found the farmer and introduced himself by his official title, he proceeded to make out as strong a case for the railroad as possible, with the hope of inducing the homesteader to be satisfied with a small payment for his loss.

"Mr. Swanson," he said with a winning smile, "the company wants to be absolutely fair with you in this matter. We deeply regret that your cow should have met her death on our tracks. But, on the other hand, Mr. Swanson, from our side there are certain things to be considered. In the first place, that cow had no business straying on our right-of-way, and you as her owner should not have permitted her to do so. Moreover, it is possible that her presence there might have caused a derailment of the locomotive which struck her and a serious wreck, perhaps even involving loss of human life. Now such being the case, and it being conceded that the cow was, in effect, a trespasser on our property, what do you think, man-to-man, would be a fair settlement between you and the railroad company?"

For a moment Mr. Swanson pondered the argument, then, speaking slowly and weighing his words, he delivered his ultimatum: "I bane jus' a poor Swede farmer," he said. "I shall give you two dollars."

★ ★ ★

A young Swede appeared at the county judge's office and asked for a license.

"What kind of a license?" asked the judge. "A hunting license?"

"Oh, no," was the answer. "Aye tank aye bane hunting long enough. Aye want a marriage license."

★ ★ ★

A Scotsman on his first visit to London got off the train and proceeded on foot to the hotel. Enroute he suffered a great misfortune. He dropped a sixpence and it rolled out of sight. The Scotsman put his luggage down and began a vigorous search for the missing coin. Soon a friendly bobby came along, and when he learned what the trouble was, he started to help him in the hunt, but with no result except for the loss of fifteen minutes. Finally the bobby said, "You go along on your way and I'll keep my eye open for your money. If it turns up I'll have it for you, if you'll come back this way this afternoon."

All day the Scot was afflicted with distress. Promptly at four o'clock he was back on the spot where his sixpence had vanished. During the day the gas company had had a squad of men excavating in the street for new mains, so when the Scotsman reappeared he found the paving torn up and a deep trench extending from the house line to the middle of the road. He gazed at the scene for a moment and then remarked to himself, "Weel, I must admit one thing—they are verra thorough here in London."

A Scotsman who had been presented with a flask of rare old whiskey was walking home briskly when a car came along which he did not sidestep quite in time. He got up and was limping down the road when he noticed that something warm and wet was trickling down his leg.

"Oh, Lord," he exclaimed, "I hope that's blood!"

HERE AND THERE

It happened during the religious wars in the sixteenth Century. During some of the roughest of the fighting, two Swedes and a Norwegian were captured by the Prussians. After spending two weeks in the local cooler they were taken out to be hanged. The execution site was at a river bank, and the platform was extended over a fastmoving river.

The first to walk up the fateful steps was Gus Jonson, one of the Swedes. The noose was slipped over his head, he stood erect, the door was tripped and he fell to his apparent death. However, the noose was too loose and he fell into the river and managed to escape in the fast-moving current.

The second Swede moved up the steps and had the hangman place the noose over his noble head. The very familiar procedure was followed once again, and lo and behold the same thing happened. He hit the water with a splash and disappeared in the water, apparently making his way to freedom.

The Norwegian was next on the program. He reluctantly made his way up the steps, and the hangman prepared to place the noose over his head. However, before he could perform the ritual, the Norwegian leaned over to the executioner and asked simply, "Would you mind tightening up that noose a little. I can't swim."

★ ★ ★

A Chinaman and an American were discussing the customs of their countries.

"I hear that when a Chinaman dies they cook a pot of rice and a mess of chop suey and put it on top of the grave," said the American.

"Yes, we do that. But you have funny customs too. You put flowers on the grave."

"That's right, we do. Tell me something, Wun Lu. When do you think the Chinaman gets up and eats all that food?"

"The same time the American gets up to smell your flowers."

★ ★ ★

The story is told of the big Swede lumberjack who bought a brand new chainsaw and was told it could cut down at least 100 trees a day.

But on the first day he only managed to cut down 25 trees. The next day he tried harder and finally cut down 33 trees. The third day he started early, worked late, and even cut his lunchbreak short, but he still managed to cut down only 48 trees.

He went back to the store and confronted the manager with his complaint. He told him of his efforts and of the results. The manager couldn't quite understand what had gone wrong, so he asked to take a look. He grabbed the starter rope and pulled hard, and the motor started with a roar.

The Swede jumped back in alarm and yelled, "Hey, what's dat big noise?"

★ ★ ★

Chung Foo Wong was the perfect Chinese houseboy in every respect but one: he couldn't seem to remember to knock on the door before entering a room. As a result he had embarrassed his comely employer time and again by barging into her boudoir when she was in various stages of dress.

She finally threatened him with instant dismissal if he ever again repeated his offense, and a whole month went by without a single intrusion by Chung Foo. "See?" beamed his employer. "It's easy enough to respect my privacy if you only put your mind to it. How have you remembered?"

"Velly simple," answered Chung Foo. "Before me come in, me look thlough keyhole. If missie no dlessed, me no come in."

★ ★ ★

The dictator of a small country was bitterly disappointed that nobody would use the newly issued postage stamps bearing his portrait. He questioned a postmaster, who explained that the stamps weren't sticking.

Seizing one, the dictator licked it and stuck it to an envelope. "Look!" he shouted; "It sticks perfectly!" The postmaster faltered for a moment, then explained, "Well, sir, the truth is that the people have been spitting on the wrong side."

Chapter 9

KIDS, KIDS!

Five-year-old Betty was constantly being irritated by her three-year-old brother, Peter, who was always getting into her toys. One day, finding that he had scattered her dolls all over the floor, she lost her patience and began to shout at him.

"Now, now, Betty," her mother soothed. "You must be nice to little Peter. Remember, God sent him to us from heaven."

"I don't think he was sent," Betty replied angrily. "I think he was pushed!"

★ ★ ★

A small boy was so imaginative that he frequently told tall tales which were far beyond the exact truth. One day he rushed into the house excitedly and told his mother he had just seen a bear in the back yard. "Now, Bobby," said his mother, "you know it wasn't a bear, it was just a big dog. I want you to go up to your room and kneel down and pray to God to forgive you for telling a lie."

After a few minutes the boy came downstairs again.

"Did you ask God to forgive you?"

"Yes, and He said it was all right. He said He thought it was a bear Himself when He first saw it."

★ ★ ★

Did you hear about the new best-seller, "Everything You Always Wanted to Know About Sex, But Were Afraid to Ask Your Children"?

★ ★ ★

Did you hear about the mean little kid who killed his father and mother and then pled with the judge for clemency on the grounds that he was an orphan?

★ ★ ★

Three little boys were lined up in front of the juvenile court judge. "Now what did you do wrong, boys? Just tell me in your own words."

"I stole potatoes from Mr. Simpson, threw broken boy, "and I threw broken glass on the highway, and I threw Peanuts into the lake."

"Now you know that's not right," said the judge. "You shouldn't do that." He turned to the second boy. "What did you do?"

"I stole potatoes from Mr. Simpson and threw glass on the highway, and threw Peanuts into the lake."

"Never do that again," said the judge, and he turned to the third little boy. "And what did you do?"

"Well, I stole potatoes from Mr. Simpson and threw broken glass on the highway."

"And didn't you throw peanuts in the lake?" asked the judge.

"No, sir," said the boy. "You see, I'm Peanuts."

★ ★ ★

Two very small boys were playing marbles together when a very pretty little girl walked by. One of the boys exclaimed fervently to his pal, "Brother, when I stop hating girls, she's the one I'm going to stop hating first!"

★ ★ ★

The five-year-old was arguing with the four-year-old.

"I ought to know," said the five-year-old. "Don't I go to school, stupid?"

"Yes," replied the other, "and you come home the same way."

★ ★ ★

He came home from school the other day and said, "Mother, I had a fight with another kid—he called me a sissy."

His mother said, "What did you do?"

He said, "I hit him with my purse."

★ ★ ★

The teacher was explaining the wondrous things which science has discovered about the universe. "Just think!" she exclaimed. "The light we need comes all the way from the sun at a speed of 186,000 miles per second. Isn't that almost unbelievable?"

"Aw, I dunno," retorted one unimpressed youngster; "after all, it's downhill all the way."

★ ★ ★

Dick: "Mom, can I go out and play?"

Mom: "With those holes in your socks?"

Dick: "No, with the kids next door."

Little Willie, the nastiest brat in the whole neighborhood, came home from his first day in the second grade. "I hope you didn't cry today," said his over-indulgent mother.

"Of course I didn't cry," sneered Willie, "but, oh boy, the teacher sure did!"

Little Percy's mother had allowed her precious child to attend public school. She gave the teacher a long list of instructions.

"My Percy is a very sensitive child," she explained. "Don't ever punish him. Just hit the boy next to him. That will frighten Percy."

Teacher: "Give me a sentence with a direct object."

Pupil: "Teacher, everybody thinks you are beautiful."

Teacher: "Why, thank you, but what is the direct object in that statement?"

Pupil: "A good report card next month."

Mother: "Did you thank Mrs. Smith for the lovely party?"

Small daughter: "No, I didn't. The girl ahead of me thanked her, and Mrs. Smith said, 'Don't mention it,' so I didn't."

LETTERS FROM CAMP

Dear Mom: Last night a mad hermit killed all the kids in camp. Your late son, Percy.

Dear Mom: I got fined for being late to breakfast this morning. I guess I overwashed. Love, Nancy.

Dear Dad: We took a couple of long hikes this week. Please send my other sneaker. Donald.

Dear Dad: We are going on a ten-mile hike. Please send my bicycle. Paul.

Dear Mommy: My counselor sleeps all day like Daddy. Love, Chris.

Dear Dad: Remember when my counselor came to visit us in the city before camp started and he said he liked little boys like me? Well, he doesn't. John.

Dear Mom and Dad: I have joined the boxing club. This morning I had my first fight. I don't think I will need braces for my teeth anymore. Love, John

Dear Folks: Yesterday our counselor told us all about where babies come from. You lied to me. Love, Margaret.

Dear Folks: What is an epidemic? Love, Tom.

★ ★ ★

Chapter 10

WORDS OF WISDOM

WITTY SAYINGS WITH A MESSAGE

We never do as well as we expect to, but the better we expect to do, the better we actually do.

A failure now and then won't harm you unless you start blaming them on someone else.

Imagination was given to man to compensate for what he is not. A sense of humor was given to console him for what he is.

When will we learn to estimate the importance of a man not by his income but by his output?

Yesterday is gone forever, tomorrow is never here, and the only time we have is today. If we have any good intentions we better put them into effect today.

Lying covers a multitude of sins—temporarily.

★ ★ ★

Some people give according to their means; others according to their meanness.

★ ★ ★

Not even a mule can get ahead by kicking.

★ ★ ★

Sympathy is two hearts tugging at the same load.

POTENT WORDS OF WISDOM

Dieting is the penalty you pay for going over the feed limit.

★ ★ ★

Times are getting tough—it used to be wine, women, and song. Now it's Metrecal, same old gal, and sing along with Mitch.

★ ★ ★

Getting up in the morning is a matter of mind over mattress.

★ ★ ★

A youthful figure is what you get when you ask a woman her age.

★ ★ ★

You can easily detect a lawyer who settles wills—He grins from heir to heir.

While a girl is single, she has to stay up half the night waiting for her boyfriend to go home. After marriage, she does the same thing waiting for him to *come* home!

A budget is a plan that enables you to pay as you go—if you don't go anywhere!

A procrastinator is someone who puts off until tomorrow the things he's already put off until today.

WISE WORDS

We learn wisdom from failure as much as from success.

Coming together is a beginning; keeping together is progress; working together is success.

Fault-finders do not improve the world; they only make it seem worse than it really is.

Seize your opportunities as they come, and you will not have to chase after them as they go.

Even the most miserable of men grow hopeful when they see a happy face. Keep smiling.

Some folks speak as they think—and some oftener.

The strong aspire; the shrewd conspire; the weak expire.

Always make the best of what little you have.

A common mistake is to ask of life more than you have put into it.

When success turns a man's head, he faces failure.

Life is full of dangerous crossings, and Conscience is the flagman.

Success simmers down to this: making the most of what you are with what you've got.

The trouble with too many of us is that in trying times we quit trying.

I WISH I HAD SAID THAT

If you could kick in the pants the fellow responsible for most of your troubles, you wouldn't be able to sit down for six months.

The brain is the only part of the human machine that doesn't wear out. Maybe it's because it's the only part that's never overworked.

Common horse sense is just stable thinking.

Be sure your brain is working before you throw your tongue into high gear.

Some people are like the bottom number of a fraction. The bigger they try to be, the smaller they really are.

A philosopher is a person who doesn't care what side his bread is buttered on because he is going to eat both sides anyway.

Most women have two views of a secret. Either it's not worth keeping or it's too good to keep.

The family tree is worth bragging about if it has consistently produced good timber and not just nuts.

Some people cause happiness wherever they go; others whenever they go.

It isn't the size of the dog in the fight, but the size of the fight in the dog, that determines which one wins.

The fellow everybody likes, generally likes everybody.

Any live wire would be a dead one without the right connections.

PROVERBS TO CHALLENGE YOUR IMAGINATION

All traffic lights on the Road to Ruin turn green when they see a fool coming.

The fellow who toots his horn loudest is generally in a fog.

Memories embellish life, but forgetfulness alone makes it bearable.

Adverse criticism from a wise man is more to be desired than the enthusiastic approval of a fool.

If some of us were to get what we really deserve, we might know what trouble really is.

Success is getting what you want—happiness is wanting what you get.

TRYING is a masterkey that will unlock any door in the world.

How easy it is to do depends on how hard you're trying to do it.

If a real go-getter found a worm in his apple this morning, he'd have fish for dinner tonight.

Sooner or later the man with pull is ousted by the man with push.

The worst boss any person can have is a bad habit.

More men get crooked by dodging hard work than become bent by honest toil.

No matter how stony the path, some move to the front, and no matter how easy the going, some lag behind.

WISE WORDS ABOUT WOMEN

A good woman inspires a man; a brilliant one interests him; a beautiful one fascinates him; but it's the sympathetic woman who gets him.

This is definitely a woman's world. When a man is

born, people say, "How is the mother?" When he marries, they say, "What a lovely bride!" And when he dies they say, "How much did he leave her?"

A devoted wife is always anxious to get home to her husband. She is afraid he may be enjoying her absence.

The right kind of woman will either make some man a good wife or him a good husband.

Nothing annoys a man more than to have his wife introduce him to her friends as though she were saying to them, "Meet my big mistake."

Marriage is an educational institution in which a man loses his bachelor's degree without acquiring a master's.

A woman feels better after a good cry because it either gets a lot of pent-up emotion out of her system or whatever it is she wants out of her husband.

The woman who thinks no man is good enough for her may be right, but more often she is left.

Marriages may be made in heaven, but they get down to earth in a hurry.

The trouble with many wives is that they'd rather mend your ways than your socks.

FOOD FOR THOUGHT

Don't just listen to what you like to hear.

A golden heart is better than a silver tongue.

If you do the best you really can, you'll find it hard to beat.

Those who depend on the breaks to win usually go broke.

Many people lose the race by hunting for shortcuts.

He gets nowhere who has no faith in his own decisions.

Every fact you learn becomes a key that unlocks a storehouse of other facts.

Life is more digestible if it is sipped, not gulped.

You can't act right if you think wrong.

He whose wants are few will not lack for possessions.

He who thinks before he acts makes one step do the work of five.

Every good thing has its price, and there is always something you must give up to get it.

Believe you can do a thing, and it's already half done.

When in doubt what to say, take a chance on getting by with the truth.

The best advice—don't give it!

TRUTH IS STRANGER THAN FICTION

Always behave like a duck—keep calm and unruffled on the surface but paddle like the dickens underneath.

Some men court trouble while others just go right ahead and get married.

All a woman needs to be successful is two good lines—one a man can listen to and one he can look at.

What is intended as a little white lie often ends up as a double-feature in technicolor.

Just about the time you think you can make both ends meet, somebody moves the ends.

Many a man in love with a dimple makes the mistake of marrying the whole girl.

Some minds are like concrete—all mixed up and permanently set.

It's all right to hold a conversation, but you should let go of it now and then.

The crank used to be in front of the old-fashioned car. Now he's behind the wheel.

A hearty laugh and a sunny smile combine into the cheapest medicine known.

Grandfather had a farm, his son had a garden, and his grandson has a can opener.

Most girls want a man with a future, while an old maid wants a future with a man.

HOW ELSE WOULD YOU SAY IT?

The more we study and read, the more we discover our ignorance.

It's easy to find fault when the fault is not yours.

The rule is not to look for big ideas from a swelled head.

There is a lot to say in her favor, but the other is more interesting.

If you are ever in doubt about kissing a girl, give her the benefit of the doubt.

Money isn't everything, but it helps until something better comes along.

The less a man knows, the longer it takes him to tell it.

Almost any girl can figure, but it's the girl with the figure who counts.

You can tell how healthy a man is by what he takes two at a time—stairs or pills.

There are a powerful lot of strings in a man's life—apron, heart, purse, and harp.

If you are not afraid to face the music, you may one day lead the band.

★ ★ ★

There's no fool like an old fool, unless it is a young one.

★ ★ ★

A wedding ring is like a tourniquet—it stops your circulation.

WORDS TO LIVE BY

When all is said and done, there's a lot more said than done.

★ ★ ★

The tighter a man gets, the looser becomes his tongue.

★ ★ ★

The man who sings his own praises is usually offkey.

★ ★ ★

If a man wants to make a fool of himself, he will always find plenty of help.

★ ★ ★

So live your life that when one evil tongue speaks ill of you, a thousand will sing your praise.

People who think too little usually talk too much.

The most effective sermon is one given by a good example.

Another thing we don't like about the school of experience is that we have to work our way through.

Wisdom is knowing what to do, skill is knowing how to do it, and virtue is doing it.

The wisest words are those a fellow doesn't say when he's angry.

It is a wise man who knows the company to keep away from.

He is set for a fall who tries to appear what he isn't.

A true smile spreads joy—a false one irritates.

You're going too fast if you can't stop when you want to.

SENTENCE SERMONS

Many people pray like kids who knock at doors and then run away before an answer comes.

Throwing mud at a good man only soils your own hands.

Do unto others as though tomorrow you would be the others.

The right angle from which to approach any problem is the try angle.

What if the way up is slow and tedious, so long as you're rising? To be climbing—that's the thing.

Peace conferences fail to abolish war for the same reason that prayer meetings fail to abolish sin—those who ought to attend them won't go.

Don't worry too much about what lies ahead. Go boldly forward as far as you can see, and when you get there you will see further.

None of us is responsible for all the things that happen to us, but we are responsible for the way we act when they happen.

Progress always involves risks. You can't steal second base and keep one foot on first.

Life is a grindstone, and whether it grinds a man down or polishes him up depends on the stuff he's made of.

You have your machinery in reverse when you try to raise yourself by lowering somebody else.

SHARP WORDS FOR SHARP READERS

We grumble about things we want to do but can't, instead of doing things we could but don't.

No matter how stony the path, some forge to the front, and no matter how easy the going, some lag behind.

It is much easier and less costly to build straight boys than to reclaim crooked men.

Marriage depends on the fusion of two lives, but it often ends with confusion.

If you don't enjoy what you have now, how can you be happier with more?

Admire those who attempt great things, even though they fail.

If you want to do it you'll find a way; if not you'll find an excuse.

What many of us need most is a vigorous kick in the seat of our can'ts.

The proper place to start curbing the crime wave is not in the electric chair, but in the high chair.

"The Man of the Hour" is generally one who has made every minute count.

The main difficulty with most of us is to make our earning power keep pace with our yearning power.

What a wonderful world this would be if we would do as well today as we expect to do tomorrow.

TEN-SECOND SERMONETTES

The business of building a life is the most important business in any man's life.

No man can add to his greatness by belittling others.

Share happiness whenever you can; it's a privilege which pays dividends.

A good deed is a blessing in disguise.

God will look you over, not for medals, diplomas or degrees, but for scars.

If some of us practiced all we preached, we'd work our fool selves to death.

The Creator made us with two ends—one on which to sit, the other with which to think. Our success depends upon which end we use the most. Heads we win, tails we lose.

★ ★ ★

Sow a thought, you reap an act;
Sow an act, you reap a habit;
Sow a habit, you reap a character;
Sow a character, you reap a destiny.

★ ★ ★

Don't worry about opposition, for it is a help instead of a hindrance. Planes rise in the air against, not with, the wind.

★ ★ ★

He is a rich man who has friends who come in when everyone else goes out.

★ ★ ★

Don't fret and worry about the future. Do what you know you ought to do today. The rest is God's affair. He has promised to be with us all the way. What more can we ask for?

★ ★ ★

Pray for the best but prepare for the worst. Note that even churches are equipped with lightning rods.

FOOD FOR THOUGHT

It is folly to worry over mistakes that cannot be corrected; it is wisdom to make up your mind to do better next time, and let it go at that.

A thimbleful of common sense and a barrel of application will accomplish more than a carload of weakly applied brilliance.

Keep your fears to yourself; share your courage with others.

You can accurately gauge the caliber of a man by noting how much it takes to discourage him.

Every outstanding success is built on the ability and eagerness to do better than just "good enough."

The fellow who falls down on the job will be back on his feet a lot quicker than the one who lies down on it.

The clock that strikes the loudest doesn't always keep the best time.

Doing a job is like shaving—the longer you put it off, the harder it becomes.

A man must believe in himself before he can get anything useful out of himself.

A man may fail many times, but he cannot be called a failure until he starts blaming someone else.

To find the caliber of a man's mind, give him some authority.

If he has a big mind, authority goes to his heart.
If he has a little mind, authority goes to his head.

The smallest package in the world is a person wrapped up in himself.

POTENT WORDS OF WISDOM

To win and keep friends, be one.

Advice after misfortune is like medicine after death.

Whatever is worth doing at all is worth doing well.

The truth never hurts—unless it ought to.

It is a mark of intelligence, no matter what you are doing, to have a good time.

The successful man lengthens his stride when he discovers that a signpost has deceived him; the failure looks for a place to sit down.

The more a wise man knows, the less he is sure about.

The hardest thing to give is in.

The ignorant are generally the most satisfied with themselves.

He who delivers the goods is never long out of a job.

Blessed is the man who has outlived the follies of his youth.

Faith is a wheelbarrow; when pushed it moves.

Don't ask God to do for you things you should do for yourself.

You can't always size up a man by the way his neighbors talk about him.

No beauty shop can duplicate a pleasant smile.

ISN'T THAT THE TRUTH!

There are many times when you cannot find help, but there is no time when you cannot give it.

Talk is cheap because the supply always exceeds the demand.

There are three kinds of workers. For example, when a piano is to be moved, the first type gets behind and pushes, the second pulls and guides, and the third grabs the piano stool.

A pessimist is someone who in every opportunity sees a difficulty, and an optimist is someone who in every difficulty sees an opportunity.

There is always plenty of sunshine somewhere, but it won't seek us out. It is up to us to find it and move into it.

Don't worry if your job is a little bigger than you are. Every important job in this world has had to be tackled by somebody who wasn't quite up to it.

Most folks are unhappy because they don't get what they want. The happy folks are those who don't always get what they want but are happy over whatever good they get.

We can't do everything at once, but we *can* do *something* at once.

Good deeds speak for themselves. The tongue only interrupts their eloquence.

When a person knows exactly what he aims to do, and goes about it resolutely, the job is already half done.

CAN YOU THINK OF A BETTER WAY TO PUT IT?

Sometimes a man keeps his nose to the grindstone so his wife can turn up her nose at the neighbors.

★ ★ ★

A gossip is a person who talks to you about others; a bore is one who talks to you about himself; a brilliant conversationalist is one who talks to you about yourself.

★ ★ ★

Good advice: the longer the spoke, the greater the tire.

★ ★ ★

The kind of friend all of us want when the clouds hang dark and threatening is not the cheerful idiot who sings, "Oh, it ain't gonna rain no mo," but the dour, thrifty, trusting one who will lend us an umbrella.

★ ★ ★

The majority of failures are not those who tried and didn't succeed, but those who were afraid to make a beginning.

★ ★ ★

Do the very best you can today—it may help you to do better tomorrow.

Cheer up—if somebody ridicules you, he is only trying to whittle you down to his size.

The man who expects much from himself and little from others has few rivals.

Overestimating your ability may lead you to a fall, but underestimating it robs you of the nerve to make a start.

It doesn't do much good to hope for success—you've got to hop for it.

Success is the ability to get along with some people—and ahead of others.

IT ONLY HURTS WHEN I LAUGH

By the time a family acquires a nest egg these days, inflation turns it into chicken feed.

Spoiled kids are the result of parents trying to raise their kids without starting at the bottom.

The greatest drawback to a budding love affair is the blooming expense.

Love has been called many things, but it'll always remain just one silly thing after another.

When some girls think of marriage, they hope their ship will come in, but usually all they get is a raft of kids.

When a girl's figure is shipshape, there are a lot of guys who want to be her first mate.

To a lot of us, reducing is nothing more than wishful shrinking.

You have to hand it to our wives—they'll get it anyway.

A honeymoon is that quiet interval between bells and bills.

No matter how much girls try to improve on Mother Nature, they're not kidding Father Time.

THAT'S A GOOD WAY TO PUT IT

Morale is something that keeps your feet going when your head says you can't take another step.

Influence is what you think you have, until you try to use it.

It may be bad etiquette for a husband to walk between his wife and the shop windows, but it's good strategy.

What a quiet, pleasant world this would be if those who have nothing to say would refrain from saying it.

If you want to see 90, better not look for it on the speedometer.

Jealousy is so instinctive in the feminine breast that no doubt Eve counted Adam's ribs every night to make sure he was true to her.

The fellow with money to burn eventually meets his match.

The road to a man's heart may be through his stomach, but the road to a woman's heart is more often a buy-path.

A gal and an auto are much alike. A good paint job conceals the years, but the lines tell the story.

The salesman whose pants wear out before his shoes is making too many contacts at the wrong place.

Even if you are on the right track, you will be run over if you just sit there.

The person who brags about what he is going to do tomorrow was probably doing the same thing yesterday.

SHORT BUT SWEET

If you don't think girls are dynamite, try dropping one.

Money can't buy happiness, but it helps you look for it in a lot more places.

A man never knows what real happiness is until he gets married—and then it's too late.

A little learning is a dangerous thing—just ask any kid who comes home with a bad report card.

A vacation is when you sometimes trade good dollars for bad quarters.

A politician is a man who stands for what he thinks others will fall for.

Remember this—when a youngster hears a dirty word, it goes in one ear and out the mouth.

Middle age is when work is a lot less fun and fun is a lot more work.

The only man who doesn't step on somebody's toes is standing still.

The forests would be very quiet if all the birds were quiet except the best singers.

SHORT BUT POTENT

The successful man makes steppingstones out of difficulties.

One foot on the brake beats two feet in the grave.

The right of free speech includes the right to refuse to listen.

The gift of laughter placed man at the head of creation.

Knowledge decreases when it ceases to increase.

Too many of those out of work want only light jobs that carry heavy wages.

There are some blessings that have to be taken away from a man to make him appreciate them.

The fastest runner cannot get away from his past.

★ ★ ★

We start by doing a lot of foolish things just for fun, and later they turn up as habits we can't shake.

No man is easier to fool than the one who knows it all.

Some people grow with authority, but others just swell.

Some men rest on the virtues of their ancestors—others stand on their own two feet.

They are already dead who say they have nothing to live for.

Four things come not back: the spoken word, the sped arrow, the past life, and the neglected opportunity.

Men are only great as they are kind.

MORE WISE WORDS

The man who is too big for a small job is too small for a big one.

Nothing is more responsible for the good old days than a bad memory.

The worst boss anyone can have is a bad habit.

★ ★ ★

Marriage is an institution that turns a night owl into a homing pigeon.

Tact is the poise that refreshes.

★ ★ ★

People who fly into a rage always make a bad landing.

★ ★ ★

A hypocrite is a man who writes a book praising atheism and then prays that it will sell.

★ ★ ★

Politicians are like ships—noisiest when lost in a fog.

★ ★ ★

Yesterday is experience, tomorrow is hope, today is getting from one to the other as best we can.

★ ★ ★

Snap judgments have a way of becoming unfastened.

You don't get ulcers from what you eat—you get them from what's eating you.

Quite often when a man thinks his mind is getting broader, it is only his conscience stretching.

What this country needs is less public speaking and more private thinking.

It's O.K. to be a self-made man if you don't consider the job finished too soon.

To grow old outside is human, to keep young inside is divine.

LITTLE NUGGETS OF TRUTH

When we're "up against it," let's remember that it's the rubbing that brings out the shine.

The best luck-piece anyone can wear is a cheerful smile.

It is well to remember that the hard work we do today will make tomorrow easier for us when today is yesterday.

We never do quite as well as we expect to, but the better we expect to do, the better we will do.

Kind words never die except when killed by ingratitude.

If you think it doesn't pay to stick together, consider the banana. As soon as it leaves the bunch, it gets skinned.

A pessimist thinks he is taking a chance; an optimist feels he is grasping an opportunity.

Keep your courage up, and it will keep you up.

Don't be a carbon copy of anybody else—make your own impressions.

It isn't advisable to tell everything you know, but it's best to know everything you tell.

Your mind is like a bank account—you can't draw out what you haven't put in.

Next time reach for the truth instead of an alibi.

TWENTY-SECOND SERMONETTES

A pessimist sees only the dark side of the clouds, a philosopher sees both sides and shrugs, a realist sees the threatening clouds and prepares for rain, an optimist doesn't even see the clouds at all—he's walking on them.

When men get too big for their britches, it's easy to fill their shoes.

Some men, like tea, never know their real strength until they get in hot water.

A happy man is one who knows what to remember in the past, what to enjoy in the present, and what to plan for in the future.

If you want to live happily ever after, don't be after too much.

If you were on trial for being a Christian, would there be enough evidence to convict you?

It's important that people know what you stand for. It's equally important that they know what you *won't* stand for.

In labors of love, every day is payday.

You can't spend yourself rich any more than you can drink yourself sober.

You can't expect a person to see eye-to-eye with you when you're looking down on him.

When a fellow is pulling on the oars, he doesn't have time to rock the boat.

HOW TRUE!

Heredity is something every man believes in until his children begin to act like fools.

Millions long for immortality who do not know what to do with themselves on a rainy Sunday afternoon.

Love at first sight was probably invented by a soldier on a two-day leave.

Nature seems determined to make us work. The less hair we have to comb, the more face we have to wash.

A specialist says that a man who sings at the top of his voice for an hour a day won't be troubled by chest complaints in his old age. In some neighborhoods he won't even be troubled by old age.

These days it is hard to tell whether a person is walking to reduce, or reduced to walking.

Some people have no respect for age unless it's bottled.

By the time you have sense enough to realize that the old folks really knew what they were talking about, you have kids who think you don't know what *you're* talking about!

Many a back-seat driver has a husband who cooks from the dining room table.

An automotive invention that is greatly needed is brakes that will automatically get tight when the driver does.

SAYINGS FROM A SAGE

Obstacles are those frightful things you see when you take your eyes off the goal you are trying to reach.

Nature is wise; in devising a man's joints, she knew he would have little occasion to pat himself on the back.

If people did no more than they have to, life would come to a standstill tomorrow.

An ungrateful man is like a hog under a tree eating acorns, never looking up to see where they came from.

Often a good scare is more effective than good advice.

Every good thing has its price, and always there is something you must give up to get it.

When success turns a man's head, he faces failure.

Adversity never made a man of anybody, but it always showed how much of a man he was.

The trouble is that we spend too much time thinking about what is going to happen, and too little time making things happen.

The supreme test of good manners is being able to put up with bad ones pleasantly.

Reputation is what you have when you come to a new community. Character is what you have when you go away.

No one ever became a howling success by just howling.

SENTENCE SERMONS

The shortest way out of a difficulty is straight through it.

We are obliged to take the world as we find it, but we ought to leave it in much better condition.

The way to succeed is to stick until you can't hold on any longer. Then take a fresh hold.

Never miss an opportunity to make others happy—even if you have to let them alone to do it.

Don't be afraid of working too hard. More people rust out than wear out.

Common sense is just the knack of seeing things as they are and doing things as they ought to be done.

To feel rich, trim your wants down to your needs.

Neither adversity nor prosperity changes a man; each merely brings out what there is in him.

What a great world this would be if we could forget our troubles as easily as we forget our blessings.

A big man is not one who makes no mistakes, but one who is bigger than any mistakes he makes.

Our grand business in life is not to see what lies dimly at a distance, but to do what lies clearly at hand.

What we say when we're on our knees is less important than what we do when we arise.

FINAL THOUGHTS

He's an ordinary type of fellow—42 around the chest, 42 around the waist, and 96 around the golf course.

The reason politicians make such strange bedfellows is because they all like the same bunk.

He has a genius for compressing a minimum of thought into a maximum of words.

The only thing the modern obstetrician has in common with the traditional stork is the size of his bill.

A fat man is seldom good at golf. If the ball lies where he can see it, he can't hit it; and if it lies where he can hit it, he can't see it.

Only a very smart man can say truthfully that no woman has ever pinned anything on him since he was a baby.

Whether it really signifies bad luck to meet a black cat depends on whether you are a man or a mouse.

Opportunity knocks only once, but temptation bangs on the door for years.

Appendix

THE IMPORTANCE OF HUMOR IN OUR LIVES

Humor as a Necessary Ingredient To Face Today's Problems

America has always been able to laugh at its problems and troubles. We find release for tensions and pent-up emotions by kidding ourselves and laughing at our dilemmas. You old-timers remember the 1930's, when we suffered through a crucial depression. We shared all types of stories involving Herbert Hoover, FDR, and the New Deal agencies, and then along came Hitler and Mussolini. They weren't very funny, but we heard plenty of jokes about them. Then remember World War II and all its traumatic developments. There has never been a four-year period of history when more humor came out. And, believe me, it helped keep our spirits up.

Recently we have gone through some real troubling times—Mr. Nixon and the whole Watergate mess, the energy crisis, inflation, crime, shortages—you name it, we have it. Good humor doesn't make the problem go away, but it does ease us over some tight spots.

Humor has been one of the great characteristics of Americans. We love to laugh and to kid each other, and even our esteemed leaders aren't spared. World travelers often relate that one impression they take away from Iron Curtain countries and Red China is the lack of laughter. Think about it! We in America are truly blessed, and I trust and pray that we will always be able to enjoy a good laugh together.

Humor as an Integral Part Of Our Human Nature

We learn to laugh soon after birth. Remember the first time your young baby gave you that smile—and then the doctor had the nerve to say it was gas! Laughter comes easy in those early years, and we all enjoy the titillating laughter of young children. Unfortunately, many people lose this gift as they mature into adulthood. However, it doesn't have to be that way.

We have several senses, and one of these is a sense of humor. I am thoroughly convinced that a sense of humor can be developed and improved, like any of our other senses. It can remain crude and primitive, or we can work to improve it to the point where it will become highly and sensitively developed. We should strive to develop our sense of humor so that we can appreciate and enjoy a comic, a joke, or any attempt at humor, even as we enjoy art, music, or drama. Obviously, a good sense of humor will become an integral part of your personality. You will find it a real asset in winning friends and influencing people.

Humor as a Necessary Ingredient For Our Physical and Mental Well-Being

Our lives today are beset by pressures and tensions which seem to grow each year. Just recently I listened to a telecast which delved into the field of mental depression and its growing problem today. Growing numbers of people are facing extreme periods of depression, which often end in physical problems and sometimes breakdowns and even suicides. Anything which can ease the tensions and relax the pressures is an important contribution to our mental and physical well-being. A healthy, mature sense of humor is obviously one of our most valuable faculties.

The ability to see the funny side of things, to laugh at ourselves and our problems, and to share some witticisms or laughs with others is truly a tremendous asset. It can help us contend with adversity, derive much greater joy out of living, and help to maintain our sanity.

Research has shown that laughter and a good sense of humor aid digestion at mealtime. It has even been proven to have a positive effect on the heart and blood pressure. Evidence is also available that people who laugh live longer than those who don't. Now for heaven's sake, don't you want to enhance your mental outlook and improve your physical well-being? Then laugh it up. Remember—he who laughs, lasts. Now don't get me wrong—a good laugh or a good joke is not going to make your problem go away; it's like sweeping the dust under the rug. Let me share a story to illustrate this point.

It seems that a Swedish rug-layer had been busy all day laying a beautiful green carpet in a lovely home in Beverly Hills. He was suffering a bad head cold, so he carried a small box of Kleenexes in his shirt pocket. He finally finished the job in the living room and looked out over the vast expanse of rug, admiring his excellent job. Then to his horror he saw a small mound in the middle of the room. He reached into his shirt pocket and, much to his dismay, the Kleenexes were gone.

He made a quick decision. He wasn't going to tear up a whole rug to rescue a lousy Kleenex package, so he gingerly crawled out on the rug and, with deft hands and a special hammer, he soon beat the mound into submission.

He crawled back and looked out on his handiwork. It was beautiful. There was no sign of the mound. He then called the lady of the house to approve the work. She came down the stairs and was overjoyed with the finished product. She then turned to the ruglayer and said, "Say, did you drop this Kleenex box? By the way, have you seen my pet parakeet?"

Seriously, I'm convinced that a mature sense of humor can have some very definite beneficial effects on your physical and mental well-being. Even the Bible gives us some wise advice about laughter. In Proverbs 17:22 we read, "A merry heart doeth good like a medicine." What clearer admonition can we find?

Humor as a Great Ingredient For Our Social Relationships

First of all, the ability to enjoy a laugh or to share an amusing tidbit does wonders for a person-to-person relationship. We love to be around a person who has a genuine sense of humor. Humor is very contagious, brightening almost any relationship. I have always regarded enthusiasm as one of the most attractive features of a person's personality. I love to be around people who are enthusiastic. In my book a good sense of humor and enthusiasm go hand-in-hand. A bubbling sense of humor has a note of optimism about it, and as a result it will almost always have a positive effect on people with whom it comes into contact.

If you have a radiant sense of humor, you will probably be the kind of person who makes friends easily. All things being equal, you are probably the kind of person who people enjoy being with. You will tend to enjoy life a lot more, and, as I said before, humor is very contagious.

This leads to social relationships in a group context. How delightful it is to have a developed sense of humor when you are thrown into a group situation. Generally speaking, you'll find a ready welcome even into a group of strangers when they sense your enthusiasm and sense of humor. How much fun it is to be the real life of the party! People look forward to your appearance because there's never a dull moment when you're around. Of course, I realize I'm looking at the ideal situation, but I still feel this can be the goal of a person who really cares.

Wouldn't it be wonderful to always leave a social group feeling that you have added to the fun of the occasion, and that those who attended are a little happier because you shared your love for humor? One caution—there is a time and a place for everything, and a person must use discretion and not be obnoxious or "hog the limelight" all the time. I think you know what I'm talking about.

Another important area where humor can be a definite asset is in your business or professional contacts. How many tensions, problems, and crises can come up in these relationships! How wonderful if you have a sense of humor to ease over tough situations, to relax tensions, or just to change the pace of a development.

There are so many places in employee-to-employee or employer-to-employee relations where a bit of humor can help solve some problems. I guess a wonderful illustration of this would be the work of Benjamin Franklin during the Constitutional Convention. In 1787 the Founding Fathers were having all kinds of difficulty in trying to resolve their differences. Every time the delegates would be at each other's throats and threatening to go home, Benjamin Franklin would ask the chairman, George

Washington, for a recess, which was always granted.

Benny would then invite the belligerents down to Millie's Tea Room for refreshments and fellowship. He'd get them laughing with stories he had brought back from Paris. Or maybe he'd share some witticisms from his Almanac, such as "An apple a day keeps the doctor away" or "Early to bed and early to rise, and your girl goes out with the other guys."

How could they be mad after they had laughed together? Back they'd go to Constitution Hall, where they would resume their deliberations. Historians have agreed that Benjamin Franklin played the great compromiser that kept the proceedings going to a happy conclusion, and wit and humor were his weapons which he used with deft skill.

What Benjamin Franklin did in 1787 is repeated daily in business offices and conference rooms all over our country. It is clear that business and professional relations can be enhanced by the generous use of humor and goodwill. Of course a sense of humor is tremendously important to any person who has to deal with people during the course of his working day.

Think of the minister, teacher, doctor, lawyer, dentist, salesman, receptionist, or waitress—and the list could go on and on. How pleasant it is to deal with a person who has a pleasing personality and a radiant sense of humor. It is a gift you cannot put a price on. This area alone could be a full-blown dissertation because of the impact it could have on the working relations in an office or a shop.

Another area in which a sense of humor plays a great role is in family relationships. It can help so much in bringing a family together. It can help in the relationship between husband and wife and between parent and child. Many tensions and difficulties arise in the ordinary, day-to-day family routine, and it goes without saying that a sense of humor can take the edge off much of the bickerings and disputes that inevitably arise. A good laugh can often clear the air, and many family problems are over minor items in the first place. Families who get the habit of integrating goodwill and humor into their family routine find fewer conflicts and tensions developing.

I have been teaching a new course at my high school entitled "The Role of Humor in American Life." I have learned a lot more than my students, I'm sure. One thing has become clear to me. There is usually a direct correlation between a student who has a keen sense of humor and the ability to use it, and the fact that he has come from a home where he has been exposed to a reasonable amount of humor in the family setting. Or let me put it this way—a youngster coming from a home where he has been happy, where humor is shared regularly with family members and where laughter is a common family trait, will have a much better chance of developing his own sense of humor to a fine point than the youngster who has been raised in a dull, morose, unsmiling, stilted family atmosphere.

Now I know that the foregoing was not a shockingly brilliant deduction, but it may help to point out that a sense of humor should be an integral part of a happy, normal home. Parents should set the pace, and their children will benefit. I believe it is possible for parents to so raise a family that their children will develop pleasing personalities which will enable them to win friends and influence people. I'm convinced that a sense of humor is an integral part of this kind of personality.